T0327162

The Emergence
of the English

PAST IMPERFECT

Past Imperfect presents concise critical overviews of the latest research by the world's leading scholars. Subjects cross the full range of fields in the period ca. 400—1500 CE which, in a European context, is known as the Middle Ages. Anyone interested in this period will be enthralled and enlightened by these overviews, written in provocative but accessible language. These affordable paperbacks prove that the era still retains a powerful resonance and impact throughout the world today.

Director and Editor-in-Chief

Simon Forde, *'s-Hertogenbosch*

Production

Ruth Kennedy, *Adelaide*

Cover Design

Martine Maguire-Weltecke, *Dublin*

The Emergence of the English

Susan Oosthuizen

British Library Cataloguing in Publication Data

A catalogue record for this book is available from the British Library

ISBN (print): 9781641891271
e-ISBN (PDF): 9781641891288
e-ISBN (EPUB): 9781641891295

www.arc-humanities.org
Printed and bound by CPI Group (UK) Ltd, Croydon, CR0 4YY

Contents

List of Illustrations

For Paul

Acknowledgements

I am grateful to Ms Sarah Wroot for drawing figures 1, 2, 3, 5, 6, and 7, and to Dr Heidi Stoner for permission to reproduce her photograph of the Repton Stone as Figure 4. I am indebted to Professor Sarah Semple for her helpful comments on an earlier draft of this book. I hope I have done justice to lessons in philosophical logic given over several years by Professor Daantjie Oosthuizen, including in particular the importance of testing the integrity of premises to arguments. And I am grateful to Mr Christopher Taylor, Dr Gordon Johnson and Professor Graeme Barker for advice and encouragement over the course of my career.

Some of the ideas explored in this volume have formed the subject of conference and seminar presentations, public lectures and university courses over the last five years and more, and I am most grateful to discussants and students who have taken the time to talk through them with me. They include, in particular, papers given at the International Medieval Congress in Leeds in July 2017 and the European Archaeologists' Association conference in Maastricht in August 2017. It goes without saying that remaining mistakes and misapprehensions are (I hope not incorrigibly) my own.

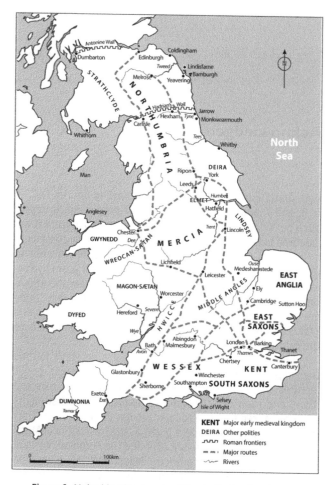

Figure 1. Major kingdoms and polities in England and Wales in the later seventh and early eighth centuries. Drawn from sources of different dates that were made for different purposes, such maps will always be approximate representing a period rather than a fixed date in time
(© Susan Oosthuizen, 2018).

Chapter 1

Introduction

One of the great puzzles of British cultural history concerns the emergence of the people who by 600 at the latest referred to themselves and their language as "English." The Greek historian Procopius, whose knowledge of late antique Britain appears to have been more than a little garbled, nonetheless knew as early as 552/3 that it was inhabited, among others, by people called *Angli*, the English.[1] In the late sixth century Pope Gregory (ca. 540–604) consistently referred to *Angli* in his letters, seemingly regarded the name as referring to the inhabitants of England as a whole since he described Æthelberht of Kent as *rex Anglorum*, "King of the English" (Figure 1).[2]

The earliest surviving documentary evidence of Old English as an active vernacular language is Æthelberht's law code written in 600.[3] *Englisc* (the English) were also mentioned in the late seventh-century laws of king Ine of Wessex (which also survive only in a ninth-century copy);[4] and the venerable Bede took both usages for granted in his *Ecclesiastical History of the English People*, the *Historia Ecclesiastica Gentis Anglorum*, written a generation or so later in about 731.[5]

Conventional interpretations of the emergence of the English and the cultural transformations of post-Roman Britain place migration into England from north-west Europe at their centre. It would be surprising had there not been migration into Britain in this period, since there has been a constant flow of people into and out of the islands since the last

Ice Age. What is less certain is what, and to what extent, that movement affected the cultural, social, and political transformations of the fifth to eighth centuries. Brugmann has neatly skewered the problem by asking, "How many migrants are needed to explain the fifth-century cultural changes generally understood as marking the transition from Late Roman Britain to Early Anglo-Saxon England?"[6]

This book explores such interpretations of the history of post-Roman Britain, the strengths and weaknesses of their supporting evidence, and an alternative model. Chapter 1 sets the scene with an overview of the prevailing historiography, necessarily limited by space. Chapter 2 distinguishes between what can reliably be known and assumed about the period, and what is more conjectural. It seeks, too, to identify flawed premises and arguments to enable the avoidance of known pitfalls and the removal of unnecessary boundaries to the kinds of questions that might be asked, despite the inevitability of making new mistakes and falling into new misconceptions. Chapter 3 takes a critical approach to ethnicity as a premise for a narrative explaining the emergence of the English, and the models based on that assumption. Chapter 4 proposes alternative, more holistic, historical models, for example, those proposed by Braudel, Bourdieu, Östrom, and Holling, and refined by others. It explores their potential through the proposition that some long-term traditions, particularly those rooted in the property rights that underpinned agricultural livelihoods, persisted into late antique and early medieval England. Those continuities, it argues, provided a strong, flexible framework that supported the gradual evolution of Romano-British into English communities between the fifth century and the early eighth century as post-imperial culture, traditions, and social relations were re-set within an international context focused on the North Sea world rather than the Mediterranean, a process in which the place of migration remains unknown. It concludes that the emergence of the English should be seen as a predominantly insular process.

Debates about the role of migration in social and cultural transformation are more than simply a pre-occupation of early medievalists, historians, or archaeologists with an interest in late antique Britain. Questions about the influence of population movement and ethnicity in stimulating and/or driving social and cultural change have an international relevance to social and political scientists both within and beyond the academy. A few years ago these appeared to be arcane problems, relegated to the dusty corners of barely attended seminars in almost-forgotten rooms. Today they are central to all aspects of public policy across the globe. They underpin discussions of social justice, of relationships within communities and between nation states, and of the courses taken by governments in steering between universal values and the narrower pressures of nationalism and populism.

The Phrase "Anglo-Saxon"

The people who occupied much of England between 400 and 1100, their culture, and the period, are conventionally described as "Anglo-Saxon." The phrase was first coined by eighth-century Carolingian writers in order to distinguish between the country of the *Angli*, in which Old English was rapidly becoming the dominant (though not sole) language, from areas on the European mainland in which other Germanic languages were most commonly spoken.[7] The term is used in the conventional division in modern scholarship of the centuries between 400 and 1066 into three general phases largely based on changing political organization: the early (ca. 400–650) Anglo-Saxon period for which there is very little documentary evidence and before the emergence of the seven major kingdoms, the middle (ca. 650–850) Anglo-Saxon period when England was dominated by those kingdoms, and the late (ca. 850–1100) Anglo-Saxon period during which England was unified within a single kingdom, notwithstanding the Viking occupation of some eastern parts of the island in the late ninth and early tenth centuries. The shorthand of the phrase makes sense: it is brief, to the point, and everyone knows what it means.

The terminology "Anglo-Saxon" is, however, beset with difficulties. The first is that it lumps together individuals whose origins lay across a wide geographic region and across at least two centuries—people who arrived between about 400 and 600 from Francia, the Low Countries, Scandinavia, and what is now Germany, north and west Africa, southern Europe, and the eastern Mediterranean. They came from within and beyond the Roman empire, spoke a range of different languages, and had diverse cultural backgrounds.[8] Even where people came from the same region, those who arrived later cannot be assumed to share a common culture or language with the descendants of earlier settlers in Britain: there are significant differences in language and culture, for instance, between modern British immigrants to the United States and the descendants of settlers who arrived there from Britain in the later eighteenth century. The implications within the phrase that fifth- and sixth-century immigrants, whatever their number, were predominantly Germanic in origin and were not assimilated into the general population is also becoming increasingly controversial, as outlined in Chapters 2 and 3 below. The apparent clarity, cohesiveness, and implied cultural identity of the phrase "Anglo-Saxon" is a chimera that shimmers into invisibility as one approaches it.

A second problem is that the phrase makes no allowance for the majority of the post-Roman population whose origins could be traced back into the prehistoric and Romano-British past and who continued to occupy landscapes familiar to their ancestors. The academic literature tends to refer to such groups as "sub Roman," "late Romano-British," or "late British" even though the period in which they lived is described as "early Anglo-Saxon." Those groups are as invisible in material culture (the things people used in everyday life) that is called "Anglo-Saxon," although they were the major users of those objects. They are invisible, too, in the name of the English language which most of them spoke by the early eighth century at the latest.

A third difficulty with an expression that construes everything in terms of being "Anglo-Saxon" is that the supposed ethnicity implicit in the phrase itself places strict limits on interpretations of the period. In taking for granted the influence of Germanic immigration on historical change it inhibits the development of other models to explain how longstanding communities adapted to post-imperial conditions, and the question of the importance of immigration in that evolution.

To avoid these problems, the period between 400 and 600 (conventionally called "early Anglo-Saxon") is generally referred to in the pages below as "late antique"; the period between 600 and 850 as "early medieval" (rather than "middle Anglo-Saxon"); and the centuries between 850 and 1066 (often rounded up to 1100), currently called "late Anglo-Saxon," as "pre-Conquest." These alternative nomenclatures are by no means perfect since they bring together two overlapping, but not coincident, frameworks for thinking of the six or so centuries after the fall of Rome.

Their strengths are that "late antique" and "early medieval" are commonly used to discuss the post-Roman development of those other parts of western Europe with which Britain remained in especially close contact after 400, in particular the areas now represented by modern Ireland, Spain, France, Italy, Germany, and the Low Countries. Their use properly places the history of Britain within the context of its wider world rather than treating it as an aberration.

Their weaknesses in relation to insular history and archaeology are immediately obvious: both those terms conventionally represent quite different chronological ranges than the three into which the evolution of Britain between 400 and 1100 is usually divided: early, middle, and late Anglo-Saxon. "Late antiquity" is usually used to denote the transition from the dominance of the Roman empire to the emergence between about 250 and 800 CE of medieval kingdoms in regions previously controlled by Rome.[9] Its use to describe a similar transition in Britain is thus appropriate for the beginning (but not for the end) of what is currently called the "early Anglo-Saxon" period, given the growing understanding of the blurring between fourth- and fifth-century Britain—for example, in the decline of villas and towns which began well before 400 in many places. "Early medieval" generally refers to the centuries between 500 and 1000 in which the origins of the Middle Ages across western Europe can first clearly be discerned; it overlaps with usages of "late antiquity." While "early medieval" may be useful for describing what is currently called the "middle Anglo-Saxon" period in England, it obviously does not conform to that wider usage. The periods into which the history of England between 400 and 1100 are currently divided make sense and they are not challenged here. At this stage a proposal to change the nomenclature itself will be controversial enough. The degree to which those terms can be refined to meet the English context is already debated; they may well be replaced by others. In that process, the periods they describe may also be redefined. How that happens will not matter so long as we can find new discourses for the history and archaeology of England between 400 and 1100 that move beyond simply discussing them in terms of the degree to which they were, or were not, "Anglo-Saxon."

Historiography

Historians and archaeologists construct explanatory models from fragmentary, more or less opaque evidence refracted through the complexities of time, place, and process. The conventional narrative for the emergence of the English that has emerged from this process subsumes so many unexplored preconceptions, premises, and arguments that it has become a paradigm: a comprehensive discourse for explaining the past whose assumptions are no longer questioned. That is in part because it has a particularly long history and because, throughout its evolution, its central conclusion has largely been predicated on its principal premise: that incoming north-west European immigrants and/or their descendants played a defining role in the almost complete disappearance of Romano-British culture, including its agricultural landscapes, and its replacement by Germanic institutions, artifacts, landscapes, and traditions.

The bare bones of the story of the origins of the English are so well known as to appear incontrovertible. They are backlit by the preceding four hundred years during which Britain was a part of the Roman empire. The Roman conquest of Britain in 43 CE had been followed by a generally peaceful period under imperial administration. The introduction of a monetized market economy was supported by improvements in transport infrastructure, the establishment of urbanized commercial and administrative centres, and an expansion in specialized production, especially of arable crops, in a largely agricultural economy. Conditions were sufficiently stable for the country's population to have grown to around three million by the early fifth century.[10] Most lived in rural settlements—often nucleated, never defended—that were closely distributed across the landscape.[11] Soon after 400, the empire, having ruled Britain for just under four centuries, withdrew its armies and civil administration from the island. Raids and other attacks mostly by Picts (from Scotland) and Scots (from Ireland) but also by Saxons (anyone from beyond Rome's north-west European frontier) that had begun in the late fourth century continued into the fifth. By the early fifth century, immigrants from north-west Europe had begun to settle in eastern and south-eastern England in a population movement that continued until the end of the sixth century.[12] As towns dwindled in size and Roman coins ceased to be imported, urban markets for surplus and specialized goods disappeared and households were forced to adopt a more localized, subsistence strategy that included growing fewer crops and focusing more on pastoral husbandry. So influential was Germanic immigrant culture, however, that almost all aspects of daily life had been transformed in its image by about 450, especially the architecture and layout of dwellings and farmsteads, and the characteristic objects used in everyday life—from personal items like weaponry or jewellery to more generic household wares. By 600 new social hierarchies had emerged, led by an "Anglo-Saxon" warrior elite who rapidly replaced the local aristocrats who had previously led the administration of late Roman Britain. And the territorial polities into which post-Roman Britain had fragmented, many previously structured as subdivisions of Roman provincial government, had coalesced by the early seventh century into seven kingdoms that dominated England until they in turn were unified under the kingdom of Wessex in the early tenth century.

The first modern exponent of that interpretation of the history of post-Roman Britain was Edward Gibbon.[13] Building heavily on the few British and continental historical sources for the fifth and sixth centuries, the outline of his story remains familiar today: Saxon auxiliary units were raised for the defence of Britain in 449, and were soon followed by five thousand warriors in three fleets who "openly aspired to the conquest of Britain."[14] Fierce British resistance initially confined them to Kent, but was unable to contain them as further groups of colonists arrived, whose varying size and status reflected that of the "intrepid chieftain" by which each was led.[15] Over the following century the Saxons inexorably overcame the resistance of the late Roman elite and gradually extended their control across lowlands of southern, eastern, and central England. The vanquished peasantry "were reduced to servitude, and governed by the traditionary customs of the shepherds and pirates of Germany."[16] In the process "the arts and religion, the laws and language, which the Romans had so carefully planted in Britain, were extirpated by their barbarous successors."[17] By the seventh century, seven Anglo-Saxon kingdoms stood on the ruins of the Roman past.

Successive generations of historians accepted this underlying narrative which gradually evolved in the light of new evidence and theoretical advances. In 1849 Edwin Guest portrayed a predominantly wooded landscape across southern England, interpreting Wansdyke and other similar earthworks as successive frontiers between Saxons and Britons that record the latter's gradual retreat westwards in the face of overwhelming Anglo-Saxon military superiority.[18] (In Maitland's imaginative description half a century later: "the German invaders must have been numerous. The Britons were no cowards. They contested the soil inch by inch.")[19] In areas of open country, especially along the major Roman roads, the conquerors found "a scene of desolation" and were immediately able to found their own farms and settlement, although "scattered here and there must have been towns, *castella* and forests in which the wretched [late Roman] inhabitants had taken refuge, and where they still maintained themselves."[20] The consequences for all aspects of Romano-British culture were devastating as successful Saxon conquerors eliminated all physical and cultural trace of their predecessors either because they had cleared the countryside, or because they had reduced the surviving late Romano-British population to a hopeless servitude.[21] Vinogradoff explained that "the formation of intermixed holdings and open-field customs in the case of settlements and plots gradually develop[ed] out of more or less complete isolation" in what he called the "tribal period."[22] T. A. M. Bishop added colour to the thesis in 1935, making a strong case for the evolution of open-fields as settlements gradually expanded into the wilderness.[23] The distribution of individual holdings across open-field furlongs at Leighton Bromswold (Huntingdonshire) were still explained in those terms in 1989: the smallest, oldest furlongs were divided between a few, original holdings; larger, later furlongs resulted from colonization of the remaining waste as the numbers of cultivators in the community rose.[24] A belief in the Germanic origins of the medieval landscape has persisted. In 1953 Homans wrote that "the customs of countrymen [...] are primary and early, probably as old as the Anglo-Saxon invasions."[25] Hoskins, whose seminal book on *The Making of the English Landscape* has not been out of print since it was first published in 1955, was similarly sure that "compact villages, of all sizes, are to be found in all counties, dating for the most part since Anglo-Saxon times. Everywhere they were accompanied originally by the open-field system."[26] Stenton considered that fifth-century colonization was "on a scale which can have left little room for British survival"[27]; by the sixth century, he declared, groups and individuals drawn from "a group of closely related Germanic nations" had extended their control across "the great plain of central England," destroying all trace of Romano-British society and culture.[28] Some recent research continues to make the same judgement: that late Roman property rights were entirely extinguished in the fifth and sixth centuries, so that "the question is not of the presence of manors or estates in earlier Anglo-Saxon times, but of the *emergence* of rights in land and rights over land."[29]

The growing contribution of archaeology to an under-standing of the fifth and sixth centuries was constrained by the conviction that its role was largely to illustrate and add more detail to that early documentary evidence.[30] For many years, for example, archaeologists worked from the premise that the rapid adoption of apparently north-west European forms of pottery, jewellery, dress, and weaponry in the fifth and sixth centuries offered physical evidence for the Germanic migrants mentioned by Gildas in the early to mid-sixth century and Bede in the early eighth. New styles for every-day artifacts like ceramics, jewellery, and weaponry became widespread across eastern, southern, and central England in the early to middle fifth century. For some, the overwhelm-ingly Germanic character of the material culture revealed by archaeological excavation led to pessimistic conclusions about the survival of late Britons. Collingwood and Myers, for example, described how "the site of a new Saxon village" lay in "an occasional clearing in woodland, accessible by Roman road or navigable stream," in a largely unoccupied primal landscape, as "the whole structure of rural society was shattered and reformed" as late Britons were reduced to enforced servitude.[31] The distributions of these new forms of artifact were taken as the most visible markers of "Anglo-Saxon" culture, and the rapidity with which they became ubiquitous across England were interpreted as evidence of the settlers' dominance. It was on this basis, for example, that Fox concluded that Cambridgeshire south of the fens had "become Anglo-Saxon" by 450.[32] Attempts to chart the progress of the Anglo-Saxon conquest against late British survival took a range of forms. Differential distributions of Romano-British traditions of inhumation burials against the "Anglo-Saxon" practice of cremation were considered to provide "a welcome test of the areas in which a culturally negative British population was sufficiently numerous to record its otherwise invisible presence."[33] Early Anglo-Saxon domination of a "scanty and backward" population in Humberside and East Anglia was believed to be demonstrated by the introduction of cremation cemeteries in those areas; in Cambridge, by contrast, the large numbers of surviving late Britons, who continued to bury their dead, were, it was said, "sufficient to prevent an immediate adoption of more civilized habits."[34]

Leeds' analysis of the typology of early Anglo-Saxon brooches was especially influential. Believing that their distinctive styles represented immigrant groups from particular regions of north-west Europe, he proposed the coalescence of Germanic settlers into Anglian and Saxon cultural groupings after their arrival in England and felt able, on this basis, to suggest that the Angles mentioned by Bede had settled in east Anglia and along the north-east coast of England, and that Saxons had occupied the region further south along the Thames.[35] Although later work challenged Leeds's methods and his interpretations, his nomenclature persisted.[36] Maps showing the colonization of England by different Germanic groups, based on the distribution of different forms of early Anglo-Saxon artifact, were published as late as 2002.[37] In 2005 Arnold still felt able to say that "settlers predominantly from the Anglian area of Schleswig-Holstein and the island of Fyn were in mid, eastern and northern England from early in the fifth century along with some Saxons."[38] And Bartholomew remained certain that archaeology revealed "the mighty movement of peoples which took place in the early fifth century and which transformed the Britannia of the late Roman empire into the land of the Angles."[39] Even more recently, innovative research on the material culture of the period has concluded that "if the earliest cruciform brooches represent migrations, then they reconfirm an obvious concentration of newcomers in East Anglia."[40]

The consensus established by Gibbon, Guest, Maitland, and their successors has underpinned the dominant interpretations of the history of the period for over two hundred years. Artifacts, language, institutions, and the landscape were, the model suggests, aspects of a cultural package introduced by north-west European immigrants in the two centuries following the end of direct Roman administration of Britain. The earliest scholarship outlined above tended to describe it as so rapid that, by the end of the fifth century at the latest, Romano-Britons of all status were subordinate within a pervasive Germanic material culture, language, and identity deliberately imposed on them, and that stood in conscious opposition to those of late Roman Britain. More recent research tends to portray a more gradual shift from the fifth century when Britons were still unquestioningly regarded as Roman to the late sixth century when the distinctions between "Roman" Britons and "barbarians" were becoming increasingly blurred.[41]

There is a growing unease concerning the integrity of both the premises and that conventional narrative.[42] Yet there are few substantive challenges to the assumption that the cultural changes of the post-Roman centuries were, in one form or another, the consequence of immigration from north-west Europe; nor has a new explanatory model been developed. It is those *lacunae* to which this volume, necessarily restricted by its format, seeks to draw attention.

Paradigms—like the conventional explanation outlined above for the origins of the English—gain traction when they offer useful interpretations of the available evidence. Their utility becomes problematic when new material can no longer be fitted into them, or when they become a straightjacket for rather than a facilitator of explanation. Those problems are exacerbated when they remain unchallenged for so long that we forget that they are simply hypotheses offering neither certain principles nor unchallengeable truths. Eventually, the strain on the relationship between evidence and interpretation becomes so severe that the paradigm can be supported only through explanations of such complexity that they border on fiction. Such propositions include, for instance, the proposal that Germanic culture became predominant at least in part through widespread, informal sexual relationships between Romano-British women and Anglo-Saxon men, the latter culturally more adept at maintaining good relationships with their subordinates. Both those women and their children by their masters adopted Germanic language and culture, eventually leading to its dominance. There is no evidence to support any aspect of these narratives. Their development points to the significant strain placed on interpretations of English history after 400 by a dependence on the central role played by "Anglo-Saxon" immigration and ethnicity. Sims-Williams pointed to problems with the paradigm thirty-five years ago, citing the words of John Kemble in 1849: "I confess that the more I examine this question, the more completely I am convinced that the received accounts of our migrations, our subsequent fortunes, and ultimate settlement, are devoid of historical truth in every detail."[43] Was he right? Chapters 2, 3, and 4 explore that question.

Notes

[1] Procopius, *History of the Wars: Books VII and VIII*, ed. H. B. Dewing (London: Heinemann, 1962), at VIII.xx.4–8; Avril Cameron, *Procopius and the Sixth Century* (London: Routledge, 1996), 213–16; for a more recent evaluation of Procopius' reliability, see Helmut Reimitz, *History, Frankish Identity and the Framing of Western Ethnicity, 550-850* (Cambridge: Cambridge University Press, 2015), 78–80. While much of Procopius' information about Britain appears garbled, it seems possible that his knowledge of the *Angli* was based on good information, since a group of Angles had accompanied a Frankish embassy in about 553 to the Byzantine court, with which Procopius had close connections. Note, too, that all dates are current era unless otherwise noted.

[2] *The Earliest Life of Gregory the Great, by an Anonymous Monk of Whitby*, ed. Bertram Colgrave (Cambridge: Cambridge University Press, 1985), chaps. 9 and 12, also at 144–45n42. For a discussion of Pope Gregory's references to *Angli*, see Patrick Wormald, "*Bede, the Bretwaldas and the Origins of the Gens Anglorum*," in *Ideal and Reality in Frankish and Anglo-Saxon Society*, ed. Patrick Wormald (Oxford: Blackwell, 1983), 99–129.

[3] "From the Laws of Ethelbert, King of Kent (602–603?)," in *English Historical Documents c.500-1042*, ed. Dorothy Whitelock (London: Routledge, 1979), 390–93. Although Æthelberht's Laws

survive only in a twelfth- or thirteenth-century copy (*Textus Roffensis*, Rochester, Cathedral Library, A.3.5, fols 1r–3v), archaic terms embedded within the text suggest that the original was written in Old English.

⁴ "The Laws of Ine (688–694)," in *English Historical Documents c.500–1042*, ed. Dorothy Whitelock (London: Routledge, 1979), 398–407; *Die Gesetze der Angelsachsen*, ed. F. Liebermann (Halle: Niemeyer, 1903), 88–123.

⁵ Bede, *Ecclesiastical History of the English People*, ed. Leo Sherley-Price, rev. ed. (London: Penguin, 1995).

⁶ Birte Brugmann, "Migration and Endogenous Change," in *The Oxford Handbook of Anglo-Saxon Archaeology*, ed. David Hinton, Helena Hamerow, and Sally Crawford (Oxford: Oxford University Press, 2011), 30–45, at 30.

⁷ Edward James, *Europe's Barbarians AD 200–600* (London: Routledge, 2009), 123.

⁸ See, for example, Walter Pohl, "Ethnic Names and Identities in the British Isles: A Comparative Perspective," in *The Anglo-Saxons from the Migration Period to the Eighth Century. An Ethnographic Perspective*, ed. John Hines (Woodbridge: Boydell and Brewer, 1997), 7–40, at 25; see also Patrick Geary, *The Myth of Nations. The Medieval Origins of Europe* (Princeton: Princeton University Press, 2002), 37; Walter Goffart, *Barbarian Tides: Migration Age and the Later Roman Empire* (Philadelphia: University of Pennsylvania Press, 2006), 93; James Gerrard, *The Ruin of Roman Britain. An Archaeological Perspective* (Cambridge: Cambridge University Press, 2013), 180.

⁹ The phrase was first used by Peter Brown in his *The World of Late Antiquity* (London: Thames and Hudson, 1971). For subsequent usage see, for example, Ken Dark, *Civitas to Kingdom. British Political Continuity 300–800* (Leicester: Leicester University Press, 1994); Rob Collins and James Gerrard, *Debating Late Antiquity in Britain AD 300–700*, BAR British Series, 365 (Oxford: British Archaeological Reports, 2004); Fiona Haarer and Rob Collins, ed., *AD410: The History and Archaeology of Late and Post-Roman Britain* (London: Society for the Promotion of Roman Studies, 2014).

¹⁰ Martin Millett, *The Romanization of Britain* (Cambridge: Cambridge University Press, 1990), 181–86.

¹¹ Christopher Taylor, *Village and Farmstead* (London: George Philip, 1983), 64.

¹² For example, Martin Welch, "The Archaeological Evidence for Federate Settlement in Britain Within the Fifth Century," in *L'Armeé*

Romaine et Les Barbares du IIIe au VIIe siècle, ed. F. Vallet and M. Kazanski, Mémoires, 5 (Paris: L'Association Française d'Archéologie Mérovingienne, 1993), 269–78.

[13] Edward Gibbon, *The History of the Decline and Fall of the Roman Empire, Abridged in Two Volumes*, vol. 1, chap. 38, part 2 (London: Straham and Cadell, 1790), 563–67. A full historiography is not attempted here; more extensive surveys can be found in, for example, Patrick Sims-Williams, "The Settlement of England in Bede and the Chronicle," *Anglo-Saxon England* 12 (1983): 1–11, at 1–5, and in Nicholas Higham, *Rome, Britain and the Anglo-Saxons* (London: Routledge, 1992), 1–16.

[14] Gibbon, *Decline and Fall*, 564.

[15] Gibbon, *Decline and Fall*, 564.

[16] Gibbon, *Decline and Fall*, 565.

[17] Gibbon, *Decline and Fall*, 565.

[18] Edwin Guest, *Origines Celticae (A Fragment) and Other Contributions to the History of Britain*, vol. 2, 147 (Port Washington: Kennikat, 1983), 156; see also 151–52.

[19] Frederic Maitland, *Domesday Book and Beyond* (Cambridge: Cambridge University Press, 1897), 222.

[20] Guest, *Origines Celticae*, 255, my addition.

[21] Maitland, *Domesday Book*, 222.

[22] Paul Vinogradoff, *English Society in the Eleventh Century* (Oxford: Clarendon Press, 1908), 277, 476, my addition.

[23] T. A. M. Bishop, "Assarting and the Growth of Open Fields," *Economic History Review* 6 (1935–36): 26–40.

[24] Brian Roberts, *The Making of the English Village* (London: Longman, 1989), 49–51.

[25] George C. Homans, "The Rural Sociology of Medieval England," *Past and Present* 4 (1953): 32–43, at 39, my amendment.

[26] W. G. Hoskins, *The Making of the English Landscape* (London: Penguin, 1955; reprinted, with editions by Christopher Taylor, London: Guild, 1988), 45.

[27] F. M. Stenton, *Anglo-Saxon England* (Oxford: Oxford University Press, 1970), 18, see also 26.

[28] Stenton, *Anglo-Saxon England*, 10 and 28 respectively.

[29] Brian Roberts, *Landscapes, Documents and Maps* (Oxford: Oxbow, 2008), 166, my emphasis. See also Helena Hamerow, *Early Medieval Settlements: The Archaeology of Rural Communities in North-West Europe: 400–900* (Oxford: Oxford University Press, 2002), 129; Debby Banham and Rosamond Faith, *Anglo-Saxon Farms and Farming* (Oxford: Oxford University Press, 2014).

[30] For an excellent detailed summary of the archaeological historiography, see C. J. Arnold, *An Archaeology of the Early Anglo-Saxon Kingdoms* (London: Routledge, 2005), chap. 1; Barbara Yorke, "Anglo-Saxon Origin Legends," in *Myth, Rulership, Church and Charters*, ed. Julia Barrow and Andrew Wareham (London: Routledge, 2008), 15–30, at 20n32.

[31] R. G. Collingwood and J. N. L. Myers, *Roman Britain and the English Settlements* (Oxford: Oxford University Press, 1945), 452, 444; see also 447.

[32] Cyril Fox, *The Archaeology of the Cambridge Region* (Cambridge: Cambridge University Press, 1923), 27.

[33] Collingwood and Myers, *Roman Britain and the English Settlements*, 449; see also E. T. Leeds, "The Distribution of the Angles and the Saxons Archaeologically Considered," *Archaeologia* 91 (1945): 1–106.

[34] Collingwood and Myers, *Roman Britain and the English Settlements*, 449.

[35] E. T. Leeds, "The Distribution of the Angles and Saxons Archaeologically Considered," *Archaeologia* 91 (1945): 1–106, at 2, 3, and 77–85.

[36] Margaret Faull, "Roman and Anglian Settlement Patterns in Yorkshire," *Northern History* 9, 1 (1974): 1–25; Julian Richards, "Cottam: An Anglian and Anglo-Scandinavian Settlement on the Yorkshire Wolds," *Archaeological Journal* 156, 1 (1999): 1–111; Brian Roberts and Stuart Wrathmell, *Region and Place* (Swindon: English Heritage, 2002), 72–77; Julian Richards, Steve Ashby, Tony Austin, et al., "Cottam, Cowlam and Environs: An Anglo-Saxon Estate on the Yorkshire Wolds," *Archaeological Journal* 170, 1 (2013): 201–71.

[37] Roberts and Wrathmell, *Region and Place*, at Figures 3.7, 3.8, 3.9.

[38] Arnold, *Early Anglo-Saxon Kingdoms*, 23.

[39] Philip Bartholomew, "Continental Connections: Angles, Saxons and Others in Bede and Procopius," *Anglo-Saxon Studies in Archaeology and History* 13 (2005): 19–30, at 28.

[40] Toby Martin, *The Cruciform Brooch and Anglo-Saxon England* (Woodbridge: Boydell and Brewer, 2015), 178.

[41] See, for example, Thomas Charles-Edwards, *Wales and the Britons, 350–1064* (Oxford: Oxford University Press, 2013), 226–38; James, *Europe's Barbarians*, at chap. 5.

[42] See, for example, Collins and Gerrard, *Debating Late Antiquity*; Haarer and Collins, *AD410: History and Archaeology of Late and Post-Roman Britain*; Rob Collins, *Hadrian's Wall. The End of Empire*

(London: Routledge, 2012); Rob Collins, "Decline, Collapse or Transformation? The Case for the Northern Boundary of *Britannia*," in *Social Dynamics in the Northwest Frontiers of the Late Roman Empire: Beyond Decline or Transformation*, ed. Nico Roymans, Stijn Heeren, and Wim de Clercq (Amsterdam: Amsterdam University Press, 2017), 203–20; Sam Lucy, *The Early Anglo-Saxon Cemeteries of East Yorkshire*, BAR British Series, 272 (Oxford: British Archaeological Reports, 1998), at chap. 2; *Walter Pohl, Strategies of Distinction: The Construction of Ethnic Communities, 300–800* (Leiden: Brill, 1998); Walter Pohl, ed., *Strategies of Identification: Ethnicity and Religion in Early Medieval Europe* (Turnhout: Brepols, 2013). I am much indebted to Professor Sarah Semple for her emphasis on their importance.

[43] Sims-Williams, "Settlement of England," at 1.

Chapter 2

What Can Reliably Be Said To Be Known about Late Antique and Early Medieval England?

Chapter 2 asks three questions: How much evidence is there to support the conventional account of the two hundred years between the removal of imperial administration and the emergence of the great kingdoms of the middle seventh century? What can reliably be said to be known about late antique Britain and what is less certain? And what would be the consequences of adopting Finberg's incomparable maxim: "to clear our mind of preconceptions, to work forwards from the beginning, and to examine the admittedly inadequate evidence as it comes"?[44] At least, the principal explanations and interpretations of the historiography would be confirmed and we could move forward confidently from that basis. At most, we could prune out false assumptions and expectations in order to establish as solid a foundation as possible for the development of new directions for research. The critical evaluation below focuses in turn on British and then continental historical sources, and then moves to consider archaeological, genomic, and linguistic evidence.

Early British Documentary Sources

There are three early British documentary sources that offer relatively direct evidence for conditions in late antique Britain.[45] The earliest is the writings of St. Patrick who was born in about 390, while Britain was still part of the Roman empire, and who died in Ireland in about 461–463;[46] the second is the sermons of Gildas, a (probably) sixth-century monk born in northern Britain who, at the time he was writing, appears to have been living in south Wales;[47] and the third is the history of the English church, written by Bede, a Northumbrian monk, who completed it in 731.[48]

Patrick's family history, first language, and the assumptions made in his autobiographical writings all speak of the continuity of late Romano-British society and culture across the fifth century. He seems to have been born and brought up in Cumbria, whence he was kidnapped in about 406, to which he returned in 412, and where he remained for a number of years thereafter.[49] He came from a family that regarded itself as Roman—his father, Calpurnius, had a Latin name; he was a Roman citizen, the owner of a villa estate, and a local aristocrat of some standing: a *decurio*, a member of a Roman city council who had important public responsibilities. He was also part of the hierarchy of the Christian church, in which he was a deacon.[50] At least partly educated, Patrick was brought up speaking vernacular (rather than classical) Latin and later learned the Irish Celtic vernacular, perhaps Archaic Irish.[51] Throughout his life he identified Britain and Christianity with *Romanitas*, describing himself as "an exile here [in Ireland] among barbarians and pagans" (a phrase that Hanson translates as "among uncivilised nations").[52] When his family begged him to stay after he returned to them in 412, he does not suggest that they had any other motive than their affection for him. He did not say that he was needed to defend them or the region against attack, or to protect them in an environment that was insecure in any way. Instead, his reminiscences took for granted the relative stability and continuity of Romanized rural life in north-west Britain in the early to mid fifth century.

The content of Gildas's *De Excidio Britanniae* (*The Ruin of Britain*), written about a century later in the early to mid sixth century, is more fraught and contentious.[53] Surely one of the leading orators of his day, Gildas described recent events in Britain in bloodcurdling religious rhetoric whose principal aim was not to establish an accurate historical record but to relate a series of divine punishments visited by God on British kings and communities who had sinned in rebelling against the Roman empire, the Roman church, and Roman standards of public life.[54] There are three significant problems for historians in developing a history of the fifth century from his work. The first is that even the period in which he was writing remains uncertain. Higham has proposed that the work can be dated to between 474 and 484; the more usually accepted dates are between about 500 and 545.[55] The second difficulty in using *The Ruin of Britain* is that there is almost no way of identifying the dates of the only two definite events that Gildas described, nor of the people he named.[56] As Sims-Williams asked nearly thirty-five years ago, "how could a historian use a narrative which named only two datable personages of the fourth and fifth centuries," which made basic errors in ascribing dates to events, and which included no clue as to when it was written?[57] Only one of the two events Gildas mentioned is believed actually to have happened: the battle of *Mons Badonicus* whose date Gildas thought was so well known that he did not think it needed to be written down. The second is a letter that he claimed was written by the Britons to a Roman commander, Aëtius, pleading for military assistance against the Picts and Scots—*not*, notably, the Saxons— who, they were said to have written, "push us back to the sea; the sea pushes us back."[58] Historians since Bede have attempted, without success, to date the letter by trying to identify Aëtius. In a detailed examination of the text, Higham suggests that, although the supposed text and addressee of the letter were both almost certainly fictitious, there is probably some foundation for each in an oral source with which Gildas was familiar.[59] That conclusion brings us no closer, though, to a chronology for the period in which he was writing. All that can be concluded from the letter is that, at some point in the fifth century, late Romano-Britons still believed that Britain remained Roman in culture and outlook and that its continuing connections with the declining empire meant that an appeal for its military assistance might still be answered with support. The third problem with the *Ruin of Britain* is that the events it records were almost certainly not listed in chronological order. Indeed many were used twice to allow Gildas make his points from two different perspectives.[60] That is, his book was never intended as a history. It is a polemical treatise illustrated with events to support moralizing points.

Despite these failings, the *Ruin of Britain* is still regarded one of the principal sources of evidence for the deteriorating relationship between Britons and Saxons across the fifth century. It is worth, then, exploring the four main elements of that story for which Gildas's authority is most commonly cited: that Saxon troops were invited to provide military support against Picts and Scots and arrived in three ships (keels); that they "fixed their terrible claws … in the eastern part of the island"; that they extorted provisions by force; and that they were subsequently expelled by the Britons in a process described as a rebellion—that is, implying that there had been at least a partially successful attempt by the Saxons to take control of the areas where they were living.[61]

There is a general agreement that Saxon auxiliaries were hired at some point during the fifth century to augment existing garrisons in southern Britain. However, the story of the three ships in which they are supposed to have arrived is almost certainly fiction. Woolf has presented a convincing argument, based on the anachronistic usage of the Old English word *cyulis* "keels" to describe the ships (the only non-Latin word in the whole of Gildas's text), to suggest that the tale of the three ships was almost certainly a later, seventh-century, interpolation into Gildas's sermons in order to make it consistent with later Anglo-Saxon folklore.[62] The second detail from Gildas's account, that the Saxons fixed their "terrible claws" into eastern England, has also been subjected to careful analysis. Harland has pointed out that Gildas mentioned claws twice: once in relation to the suppression of attacks by Picts and Scots by Roman troops, and once in connection with the Saxon troops. He suggested that the repetition of the word was a rhetorical device counterpointing what Gildas regarded as the legitimate "claws" of imperial Roman troops engaged in defending the empire with those of late Romano-British military leaders who had illegitimately brought Saxon auxiliary troops into Britain to support them in fomenting civil war.[63] That is, Gildas was not recording a forcible act of conquest. He was making a pointed contrast between the legitimate force of the imperial army and what he considered to be illegal use of force for their own ends by those late antique British generals who employed Saxon auxiliary units in eastern England.[64] The third narrative detail commonly drawn from Gildas is that Saxon troops forcibly extracted provisions at the places in which they were stationed. Higham, however, has shown that Gildas's account simply described standard late Roman practice in conventional technical terms: The Council had raised a limited number of auxiliary cohorts [*hospites*], drawn from beyond the empire, who were billeted on local citizens and whose rations [*annonae*] were military supplies customarily raised from civilians.[65] That is, Gildas described the Saxon troops as units of the Roman army housed and provisioned in conventional ways. It is a misinterpretation of his text to characterize them as invaders or colonists. Finally, *The Ruin of Britain* goes on to describe how those troops eventually left Britain. Gildas does not say that they settled in eastern England nor anywhere else.[66] The most significant military threats he described were not from Saxons, but from Picts and Scots.[67] *The Ruin of Britain* is thus a fragile foundation for the traditional accounts of the Anglo-Saxon settlement. It cannot be used to support accounts of permanent settlement of and forcible occupation by Saxon troops, nor their subsequent hegemony, nor rebellions against them.

Gildas's text does, however, offer some evidence for the structure and quality of life in fifth-century Britain. Although he lamented that cities lay "in ruins," the decline of towns in Roman Britain had begun in the fourth century and cannot be laid at the door of the fifth—except, perhaps, in that there was then no urban regeneration.[68] He described a functioning legal system with *iudices*, courts and jails; an ecclesiastical hierarchy with bishops, priests, and subordinate clergy; and monastic houses with abbots and monks. Military command structures, units, and administration were still organized on Roman lines. The landscape was settled and productive of arable and stock. And the period before the attacks that led to the employment of Saxon units had been notably prosperous.[69] This is not to argue that nothing had changed: a once-unified province was divided between kings and kingdoms, and new political, administrative, social, and economy structures *were* evolving—but from a traditional base. The result was a gradual divergence from Roman norms of which the emergence of militarized leadership was, it seems, what Gildas most objected to.[70]

The third major source for the history of the fifth and sixth centuries is Bede's *Historia Ecclesiastica Gentis Anglorum*, completed in 731 almost two hundred years after Gildas's account was written.[71] Its clarity of structure and expression, and its attempt to establish a sound chronology for the early period—qualities the more seductive for their absence in the other sources discussed above—makes it the most highly regarded of the three insular narrative accounts. It is, however, not as useful or successful as it appears at first sight. There are two reasons for this. The first is that Gildas remained Bede's principal source and he failed in the considerable efforts he made to correlate Gildas's accounts with other evidence in order to substantiate the latter's chronology. In a devastating critique that has yet to be overturned, Sims-Williams concluded in 1983 that, for these reasons, "Bede's chronology is simply a valiant attempt to interpret Gildas and has no independent value whatsoever"[72]; his dates are "of value only for the light they shed on early Anglo-Saxon dynastic, heroic, and topographical tradition and learned historiography"—that is, in establishing the range and approach of other material that he consulted.[73]

The second reason for treating Bede's account with some care is that his narrative, however carefully it may have been constructed from documentary accounts and oral testimonies, was not free from bias. His objective, not always consistently achieved, appears to have been to establish the primacy of the church of Rome across England by discrediting the legacy and teachings of the Romano-British Celtic Christianity that predated the arrival of St. Augustine in the late sixth century.[74] On the one hand, Bede venerated the secular legacy of the Roman empire in Britain; on the other, his narrative for the ecclesiastical success of St. Augustine's mission and legacy depended on the vilification of the late Romano-British church and the society that it represented.[75] His opposition of the English and the British was thus a rhetorical construct. Whether it was based in reality remains unknown.

The reliable sections of each of these early narrative sources tell us only that evolved Romano-British administrative, judicial and religious institutions were still recognizable across Britain from Wales to St. Albans in the late fifth or early sixth centuries; that attacks—principally from Scots and Picts, but also from Saxons—that had begun in the middle of the fourth century, continued across the fifth; and that the agricultural sector remained peaceful and productive. As Higham has noted, "their survival implies the continuing existence of the fabric of lowland society and the continuing flow of goods from the producer classes to a civilian gentry in the form of both rents and taxation."[76] There was continuing close contact with the Mediterranean world through the church, through diplomatic gifts, and travel, while at the same time trade with and from regions around the North Sea grew in volume and importance.[77]

Yet even where the *minutiae* of both Gildas's and Bede's accounts are acknowledged as dubious, the general outline of the events they described has remained irresistibly attractive. It has been adopted as a cast-iron chronological framework for narratives based on fifth- and sixth-century immigrants who, within a few generations, had supplanted Romano-British society, its culture and its institutions with their own. A recent study of the emergence of early Anglo-Saxon kingdoms in southern Britain, for example, concluded that "kingdoms could be seen as the gradual outcome of competition between elites who had never lost the military prowess that apparently had made them attractive as mercenaries to the British in the fifth century, *if Gildas is to be believed.*"[78] Some genomic research similarly structures its interpretation of DNA evidence for early medieval immigration in terms of the reliability and integrity of those early sources (see "The Evidence of Genetic and Isotopic Research," below).[79] The problem with that reliance on such early documentary evidence is, of course, that neither Gildas nor Bede set quill to parchment with the aim of providing a full, neutral narrative.[80] None of these sources offers sufficient solid ground to support the case for the settlement or conquest of England by "the Anglo-Saxons."

More than a generation after it was written, Sims-Williams' biting observation remains pertinent: many researchers are still "more interested in showing how the narrative usually constructed from [Gildas], Bede or the [*Anglo-Saxon*] *Chronicle* might be confirmed, amplified or qualified by archaeological or place-name data than investigating the reliability of the primary historical sources."[81]

Early Continental Documentary Sources

There are six brief, often cryptic, references to events in fifth- and sixth-century Britain in the works of contemporary continental writers whose interests were naturally more focused on their own geographies than those of this island.[82] None stands up to scrutiny as evidence for the forcible occupation of Britain by fifth- and sixth-century immigrants from northwest Europe. Instead, they confirm St Patrick's and Gildas's accounts of the persistence of late Romano-British society and institutions at least into the middle of the fifth century.

Imperial administrators and troops were still present in Britain in 407, since Zosimus, writing in Constantinople in about 498–502, reported the mutiny of Roman troops in Britain in that year and their election of Constantine as emperor, describing how "the Britons rebelled against Rome" and "reverted to their native customs."[83] His source was a much-admired, lost history of the western empire by the renowned Greek historian, Olympiodorus of Thebes, written in around 427, only about twenty years after the events it recorded. This was the third mutiny in Britain in under two years and, although the events themselves remain murky, the election of three usurpers in rapid succession suggests considerable political instability and social unease about the unpredictability of events across the western empire. They may represent active steps by military and civilian imperial staff based in Britain to maintain what they perceived as the *status quo*.

The Roman army and administrators are assumed to have been withdrawn from Britain soon thereafter on the basis of Zosimus's account of a rebellion by "the British" against Saxon rule in about 409.[84] The passage in question is generally translated along the following lines: "The Britons, therefore, taking up arms and fighting on their own behalf, freed the cities from the barbarians who were pressing upon them."[85] Bartholomew, however, has argued that a careful examination of the entry in different copies of Zosimus's text indicates that the original Greek has been misunderstood by its translators. Rather than "pressing upon them," the phrase should be translated as "stationed" or "billeted."[86] In other words, late Romano-British leaders were not rebelling against Saxon invaders. They were acting to send home Roman auxiliary troops drawn from barbarian Europe (as many in that period were) who were billeted in their towns and under the command of Romano-British generals. As we have already seen, Gildas used the same technical terms in recording the same events. Both accounts agree, it seems, in recording that fifth-century Romano-British civilian leaders adopted the formal structures of the Roman army in organizing their forces in order to uphold what they saw as Roman norms, and that late antique political and military elites were sufficiently in control across their regions to be able to send such forces home when they were no longer required.

A second, similarly much-cited passage from Zosimus's history—also based on Olympiodorus's work—records that in about 410 the Emperor Honorius sent "letters to the cities in Britain ordering them to guard themselves."[87] That text forms the basis of the generally adopted proposition that at this time the empire effectively cast Britain adrift since it was no longer able to send troops to its defence. Bartholomew attacked that interpretation in terms not only of the accuracy of its translation, but also of its context. Both, he suggested, make more sense if Honorius's letters were sent not to cities in Britain but, instead, to those in Bruttium (now Calabria) in southern Italy.[88] He suggested that βρεττια, the Greek form of Bruttium which Olympiodorus demonstrably used elsewhere, was mistaken by later historians and copyists for βρεττανια (Britain).[89] That possibility gains force from the contemporary context within which the letters were sent: the hostilities between Honorius and Alaric, during which the barbarians threatened cities in or around Bruttium. "In the circumstances," Bartholomew concluded, "it would be rash in the extreme to try to use this passage as evidence for the fate of Roman Britain."[90]

Two further accounts of events in post-Roman Britain are found in the *Gallic Chronicle* of 452. The first records that "Britain was devastated by an [undated] incursion of Saxons."[91] It is conventionally attributed to 409-11, on the assumption that its place in the Chronicle denotes its place in an ordered chronology. The second entry is dated 441/2 and notes that Britain was lost to the empire, having come under the authority of the Saxons.[92] Miller and Bartholomew have each argued on the basis of syntax, wording and context that both were later, eighth-century, fictional interpolations introduced in order bring the *Chronicle* into line with Bede's *Historia*.[93] Burgess agrees that the events of 409-11 almost certainly never happened, but concludes that the note of 441/2 is probably comparatively accurate in recognizing that Britain was by then no longer part of the Empire; he suggests, however, that the chronicler's gloss about Saxon governance was probably hearsay, recorded by someone writing in Provence, a long way from Britain.[94] Jones and Casey, following some cautious dissent by Muhlberger, vehemently disagree with any doubts concerning the *Gallic Chronicle* and argue strongly for its historical integrity.[95] The weight of scholarship thus tends toward dismissal of the record of a revolt against the Saxons in 409-11. The degree of academic dispute concerning the reliability of the entry for 441/2, however, remains so intense that Burgess's position is perhaps the least controversial: that Britain was widely regarded as lying beyond the empire by the middle of the fifth century, but that the form and source of its governance cannot be assumed to be "Anglo-Saxon."

And finally, a visit to Britain in 429 by St. Germanus, Bishop of Auxerre, was recorded by Prosper, a Roman churchman, in 433 and in a biography of Germanus written by Constantius in about 480; both are believed to have had access to an official report on the mission.[96] The first, said Barrett, "is a source that commands respect for the factual reliability of its entries."[97] The purpose of Germanus's mission was to suppress heresy in the British church, something he is said to have achieved. The Britain of both accounts was stable and prosperous; the authority of the church of Rome was unchallenged; and Germanus was able to visit the shrine of St. Alban at Verulamium without difficulty. That political and military structures continued to frame post-imperial arrangements is suggested by the "man of tribunian authority" whose daughter Germanus cured of blindness, and by the apparent ease with which yet another joint attack by Picts and Saxons was repulsed.[98] At the end of the mission "this very opulent island found peace with security on several fronts."[99] This is not the description of a society in chaos, subject to political uncertainty or economic volatility. Instead, it confirms Patrick's portrait—significantly, in a different part of Britain—of late antique political, social, and economic stability.

There is, then, no reliable, contemporary documentary evidence from early British or continental scholars for substantive invasion, settlement, or conquest of Britain from north-west Europe in the fifth century, and at least some to support arguments for sufficient social, economic, and political stability to allow Roman administrative and military structures, with a local history of up to four hundred years in some parts of Britain, to continue to evolve and adapt across at least the first two post-imperial centuries.

Archaeological Evidence

The considerable population density across, and consequent intensive exploitation of, the British countryside from prehistory into the late antique period is now well-accepted. By 400 the population is generally held to have numbered around three million.[100] This has led to a general recognition that, since late antique Britain was largely populated by people of Romano-British descent, only a few individuals in each cemetery or settlement can have been those of immigrants or their direct descendants.[101] This means that the key premises of late nineteenth- and early twentieth-century historians and archaeologists that a militarily weak Romano-British population was killed or driven out by small, but formidable, groups of "Anglo-Saxon" invaders has been comprehensively dismissed. The assumptions of Gibbon, Maitland, and Vinogradoff that the Romano-British landscape was still largely wooded, underpopulated, and underexploited, have been comprehensively refuted by archaeological work from the 1970s onwards. Instead, lowland Romano-British settlements often lay no more than 250 metres to 500 metres apart; distances between upland settlements remained more or less the same as they had been half a millennium or more earlier, but the sizes of the settlements themselves had doubled or trebled.[102] It is now generally accepted that the fifth-century landscape was fully occupied and exploited, whether for arable or pasture.[103]

Such underlying continuities contrast with significant changes in post-Roman material culture: the forms, craftsmanship, and artistic styles of goods imported into Britain from the many places that bordered the North Sea both influenced and were absorbed into evolving insular production—cruciform brooches are just one example of an imported form that was adopted by local craftsmen under whose influence it gradually evolved.[104] Romano-British communities had been used to seeing themselves as an integrated part of a larger world, defined before the early fifth century in terms of the Roman empire to which they were connected by government, economy, and (from the mid-fourth century) the church.

The widespread adoption of elements of Germanic material culture by the middle of the fifth century suggests that that vision of being part of a wider world shifted away from the Mediterranean to embrace the region around the North Sea.[105] What remains unknown is whether these changes simply reflected changes in cultural preferences—what we would today call fashion—or whether they are evidence of immigration, or a combination of both.

Whatever the answer to that question, a growing volume of research indicates that many elements of late antique material culture combine, in varying degrees, Romano-British craft technologies and designs with the stylistic influence of goods from across the North Sea. Three examples illustrate the point. A comparison between the flamboyant loops and curves of interlace work on late antique brooches, stonework, and other artifacts, and Iron Age decoration preserved on mirrors and shields indicates that continuing traditions of prehistoric and Romano-British metalworking did not disappear after the end of Roman administration in Britain, but continued to contribute to fifth- and sixth-century (and later) aesthetic tastes. Similarly, late antique and early medieval enameling has long been recognized as persistence of a Romano-British craft tradition.[106] And again, a small group of late antique textiles called three-shed twills were woven on Romano-British looms using traditional techniques to produce traditional forms of cloth long after everything else about those who wove them appeared to be "English."[107] The apparently sharp distinction between fourth-century "Romano-British" and fifth-century "Anglo-Saxon" artifacts has been blurred by the recognition that most of the artifacts used in everyday life combined, to a greater or lesser extent, traditions of British and North Sea craftsmanship and artistic expression.

Recent research has also investigated the proposition of economic collapse after about 400. The primary cause of that collapse is usually held to be the cessation of Roman coin imports that had, it is believed, underpinned a market economy that allowed producers to sell specialized agricultural products sold for cash with which they could buy the other goods they needed or the high status artifacts that they coveted.[108] The disappearance of coins meant that those redistributive markets also vanished and agricultural producers were forced into to a highly localized, subsistence economy whose stresses eroded political stability and which resulted in shortages of food and other goods, and a sharp drop in living standards. Thus, the conventional argument suggests, even if the country was not depopulated, the consequent economic and political void offered the chaotic conditions in which Germanic warriors could impose their own leadership and their own imported political institutions on a subjected, British population.[109]

Numismatic research has begun to breach those conclusions. New discoveries and analysis of existing collections show that Roman silver and low value bronze coins continued to circulate in the fifth and sixth centuries, although the former appear to have been in short supply; and that there were smaller-scale imports of high value gold coins especially from Merovingian Gaul, and Burgundy, as well as from Visigothic Spain and other parts of western Europe, the eastern Roman empire, and even the Middle East.[110] Coins did not disappear from Britain in the post-Roman centuries, although their volume and role in commerce changed.

Other work challenges the explanation of systemic economic shock that is held to have reduced late Romano-British cultivators to a hand-to-mouth subsistence within conditions of political chaos as rival warlords tussled for control over the smaller or larger areas within which they lived.[111] Gerrard has pointed out that agricultural economy was, and remained, the largest sector in the contemporary national economy until the nineteenth century. This, he argues, suggests that its scale in the Roman period was such that it was almost certainly largely unmonetized; that is, agricultural goods were not generally dependent on the availability of coin for their exchange before or after 400.[112] In that case, post-Roman changes in the volume of coinage in circulation may not directly have affected the agricultural sector. The withdrawal of Roman administration may even have had beneficial indirect effects for producers since there was a consequent reduction in demands on them for taxes and other renders to the state.[113] Productive households could now be more flexible in setting the balance each year between crop and animal husbandry; the shift to a greater emphasis on pastoralism, while feeding fewer people per unit area, incurred lower labour and other capital costs; and farmers may have been able to retain a greater proportion of their surpluses, thereby improving rather than degrading standards of living across the fifth century and stimulating a substantially positive transformation of agriculture. Indeed, Gerrard suggests, the late Roman elite "far from feeling the pinch, may have found themselves the recipients of a greater proportion of their peasants' surplus than they had ever dreamt possible" and the peasantry themselves may also have been better off.[114]

There is some support for that position from other areas of research. Research on the manufacture and extensive distribution of high quality, wheel-thrown pottery, for instance, previously believed to have been extinguished by the cessation of Roman coins imports, illuminates the effects of post-Roman changes on markets, industrialized manufactures and their distribution after 400. Until recently wheel-thrown pottery was considered to have disappeared by the middle of the fifth century: Nene Valley ware, for instance, was produced and distributed across Britain from manufactories around Water Newton in Cambridgeshire ceased to be made towards the end of the fourth century.[115] It was believed to have been replaced by locally produced handmade pots in fragile fabrics, and that it was only two centuries later wheel-thrown ceramics were once more made and distributed on any scale anywhere in Britain.[116] A reconsideration of the evidence, alongside new finds and analytical techniques, has shown that wheel-thrown pottery continued to be produced alongside homemade wares across the fifth and sixth centuries, that it continued to be distributed from specialist centres, and that its designs evolved from Romano-British towards "Anglo-Saxon"—suggesting that at least some "Anglo-Saxon" ceramics may have been a new range, produced by traditional British manufacturers.[117]

Palaeoenvironmental evidence for changes to patterns in agricultural land-use in the fifth and sixth centuries also indicates continuity rather than disruption in daily life. Although there were some places where Romano-British fields did disappear under regenerated woodland from the early fifth century onwards—for example, in Rockingham Forest, large tracts of the Weald and the more marginal uplands of Exmoor—it was relatively rare for fields to be abandoned to the extent of reverting to a cover of dense woodland, a process that Rackham observes can take as little as thirty years.[118] Instead, most formerly arable landscapes continued to be fully occupied and utilized for grazing—that is, they demonstrate a shift from high intensity to lower intensity forms of agricultural production. Pollen evidence suggests that the size of these fifth- and sixth-century flocks and herds was large enough not only to prevent regeneration, but also to maintain a consistent mosaic of grassland species on those pastures thereafter.[119] The archaeology of faunal remains offers another similar conclusion. Results show an increase in animal protein (including the dairy products that were gained from a greater emphasis on pastoral husbandry) and a concomitant decrease in the proportion of carbohydrates in everyday diets appear to have led to general improvements in health across the board, visible in increases in average height, better dental health, and higher recovery rates from infection.[120]

Continuity in the economic function of some villa estates, once similarly believed to have been abandoned, is also now more widely recognized. Whether or not they were still places of aristocratic residence, they remained "nodal points in the landscape storing and processing foodstuffs" rendered to a rural elite.[121] The agricultural specialization that had generated the surplus that supported the sale and exchange in markets of grain, animals, and their secondary products gave way to localized production for subsistence—visible in the widespread conversion to pasture of large areas of ara-

ble; but there is little evidence that those fields were abandoned.[122] While many villa buildings gradually fell into ruin,
they or their sites frequently remained centres for continuing
activity. In some cases, buildings were repurposed by subdivision, conversion into storage, or for specialist facilities
like corn-drying, smithing, and other industrial activities; in
other places, they were replaced by wooden aisled halls built
over or alongside them; and on yet others they formed the
focus for early Anglo-Saxon cemeteries.[123] All support Gerrard's arguments for the late antique stability of the agricultural sector and the beneficial effect on peasant household
economies of the withdrawal of Roman secular and military
administration.

Roman towns, villas, and military establishments, respectively representing civilian and military administrative infra-
structures, are still widely considered to have been abandoned over the decades after 400.[124] There is, however, a
growing volume of evidence to suggest that small-scale settlement persisted in many Roman towns into the fifth and
sixth centuries and beyond. On the other hand, it seems
unlikely that that occupation could be characterized as
urban, and the numbers of towns that survived to provide
the focus for renewed urbanism in the seventh and eighth
centuries remains contentious.[125] Yet there are indications
of some kind of continuity, however slight, in the continued
functioning of Romano-British territories controlled from
small Roman towns like Great Chesterford (Essex) and Cambridge (Cambridgeshire).[126] Similar traces can be discerned
in the persistence into some of the early kingdoms of the
territories of larger *civitas* capitals like Canterbury (Kent),
based on the Romano-British *civitas* of the *Cantii*;[127] or the
kingdom of Lindsey, recorded in the late seventh century
and whose name evolved from a Brittonic to an Old English
form, which was based on the former *territorium* around the
colonia at Lincoln (*Lindum*).[128] What is the balance in argument between the collapse of urban functions visible in the
disappearance of administrative oversight of a region, the
collection of taxes, or the dispensation of justice—if the terri-

tory it had once controlled continued nonetheless to be recognized as an administrative, fiscal, and political unit? Cambridge is a notable example. The monks who came to look for a marble sarcophagus for St. Æthelthryth in 673 found a "small abandoned city."[129] Yet continuity of its administrative and other functions is suggested by the place-name of modern Grantchester, which lies within the former Roman town's *territorium*. It preserves the name of the *Granta-sæte*, a late antique administrative unit that may have controlled much of the catchment of the River Cam, whose Celtic name was Granta.[130] There are other examples; the significance of those five is, of course, their location along the east coast of England where Germanic migrations were supposed to be the most intense and the most disruptive.

The withdrawal of the Roman army from Britain in the early fifth century is held to have left former defences unmanned and undefended thus allowing Picts, Scots, and Saxons to move across them at will. Recent work along Hadrian's Wall negates that view. In a carefully nuanced assessment Collins suggests that "most, if not all, the soldiers of the late Roman frontier remained in place after Roman rule ceased in Britain."[131] That continuity of function did not mean stasis in its structure and organization. The boundary between official and domestic functions within the forts along the Wall became blurred, and there may have been a flattening in the military hierarchy; nonetheless the Wall continued to be defended, and its installations refurbished, into the eighth century.[132]

Such interpretations make the important point that other explanations for the transformations of the fifth and sixth centuries are possible, and that neither economic collapse nor consequent political instability were inevitable consequences of the contraction of the empire beyond the Channel.

There is no doubt that archaeological evidence demonstrates substantial change in the character of the material culture of fifth- and sixth-century England. It does not, however, support the old certainties of Germanic political and cultural ascendancy but offers a more nuanced, regionally variable, view that indicates the evolution of a late antique society and economy in a wider, post-imperial world. Most people in late antique and early medieval England were descended from Romano-British and/or prehistoric communities; late Roman craftsmanship, technology, and artistic expression continued to flourish after 400; many villa estates continued to be seen as centres of lordship; and there was no break in the agricultural economy. Analyses of the stratigraphy of excavations, the typology of evolving designs, the broad results of carbon dating and other methods of scientific analysis, and so on, have begun to show the way to more complex explanations of the period in which there is less dependence on the histories of Gildas and Bede. What, then, *was* the role of migration?

The Evidence of Genetic and Isotopic Research

Since there has been a consistent migration into and from Britain for millennia, the presence of fifth- and sixth-century immigrants is hardly surprising—indeed, it would be more surprising had there been no inward and outward population movement in those centuries.[133] But no-one knows whether the numbers of those who arrived in late antique Britain were higher or lower than average, or simply typical; nor what their places of origin were.[134] As Reynolds has observed, "we have very little evidence at all, outside stories that were told and elaborated after the sixth century, that a larger proportion of the population of Europe moved around during the 'Age of Migrations' *than at any other time*" or that they "were not only enduring political and cultural communities but were biologically heterogeneous too."[135]

Advances in genomic research have stimulated attempts to resolve such questions about the number of "Anglo-Saxon" immigrants arrived between 400 and 600, the places of their origin, and the parts of England in which they settled. Until recently such studies have used analyses of modern DNA to reconstruct the population history of post-Roman Britain. Their results show that most Britons can trace their ancestry back into the prehistory of these islands and that there is substantial homogeneity in modern British DNA.[136] There is no evidence of pockets of "Germanic" settlement in eastern or central England or of "Celtic" populations in the west, even in areas like Wales and Cornwall where the latter might be expected.[137] Other conclusions are more controversial, in particular that between ten and thirty-eight percent of modern English DNA is derived from "Anglo-Saxon" migrations.[138] That result has been questioned for a number of reasons. First, research methods and conclusions are sometimes skewed to fit what is believed to be known about the *adventus* rather than being based on the genetic evidence itself. So, for example, a recent major study based on modern DNA samples identified migration into Britain from northern Germany, Denmark, *and France* in the middle of the first millennium.[139] However, the authors excluded the French evidence from their interpretation of the results on the grounds that Gildas and Bede had recorded that "the Saxon migrations did not directly involve people from what is now France."[140] That is, the researchers assumed that the migrations were Germanic and then skewed their results to achieve that predicted conclusion.

A second problem is that computer simulations suggested that intermarriage between existing communities and immigrants from north-west Europe occurred in the ninth century, around three or four hundred years *after* "the Anglo-Saxons" are supposed to have arrived.[141] Kershaw and Røyrvik have suggested two straightforward solutions to that apparent conundrum. First, they have observed that the apparent solidity of the mid-ninth century date is an artifact of computer modelling which aggregates all early medieval Germanic DNA into a single data set, when it may in fact represent continuous, small-scale immigration into Britain between the late fourth and the mid-ninth centuries. In that case, the conclusion might be set aside. They also observe that, if that ninth-century date is taken at face value, it is more likely to record the Viking settlement from 870 onwards than intermarriage, inexplicably delayed for several centuries, between local communities and the descendants of fifth- and sixth-century "Anglo-Saxons."[142]

As importantly, Geary and Veeramah have critically evaluated the fundamental premise that ancient population history can be identified from modern genomes.[143] They have pointed out that sampling just one strand of an individual's genome (that is, a single ancestral line) so simplifies population history that the results may not be useful, because "almost all European individuals, even when separated by large geographic distances (>2 km), shared hundreds of ancestors within the last 3,000 years" and following a single line was likely to place undue emphasis on a limited proportion of an individual's ancestry.[144] They point out, too, that results from DNA studies in Iceland show that less than 50% of the DNA found in ninth-century Viking burials is represented in the modern Icelandic population.[145] This means that, if there were an attempt to reconstruct the Viking population from modern Icelandic DNA, half of them would be missing from the result. How useful, then, can modern genomes be in reconstructing the population history of late antique or early medieval England in order to reach conclusions about the volume and period of post-Roman immigration?

Such problems might be avoided if the genetic material of people actually living in the period under study was used instead. That premise formed the basis of an innovative comparison of four people buried at Oakington in about 500 and three eighth-century individuals from a cemetery at Hinxton (both Cambridgeshire) with Iron Age populations who lived in the area sometime between 360 BC and 0 BC/AD.[146] The difficulty with the study (beyond the small numbers of the samples) is immediately obvious. It measured change between (at worst) 360 BC and 700 AD (a period of nearly a thousand years) or (at best) between 0 BC/AD and 500 AD. At a minimum, then, the results measured immigration across the entire Roman and immediately post-Roman periods, or at most from the late Iron Age into the ninth century. As a consequence the results cannot demonstrate the extent of "Anglo-Saxon" immigration *after* the Roman period—to do that, the earliest samples would have had to have been Romano-British, perhaps from the later fourth century. So although the results show a significant overall increase in north-west European DNA between the Iron Age and the eighth century, the flaw in the method means that there is nothing to indicate they reveal people arriving in Britain specifically between 400 and 700.[147] A final complication is that isotope analysis revealed that the three eighth-century individuals from Hinxton, discussed above, were themselves immigrants from north-west Europe, underscoring the point that migration was a continuous process and making it even more difficult to place the introduction of "Anglo-Saxon" DNA in the fifth and sixth centuries, and placing the entire burden of proof on the four individuals from Oakington.[148] This is not to argue that the genetic research does not show the Anglo-Saxon migrations. Perhaps it does—but, at least as things currently stand, it may equally well not. The case must be regarded as unproven. Otherwise, to paraphrase Gerrard's inimitably blunt conclusion, we cannot discount the possibility that "the historical tail is very much wagging the genetic dog."[149]

An alternative approach has been to analyze isotopes in dental enamel which preserve information about the regions in which individuals had been brought up.[150] Growing numbers of these studies which throw the problems of genetic research into further relief since they demonstrate that newcomers—who grew up across the late Roman empire—were both small in number and assimilated into local communities. Nineteen individuals buried in a cemetery at Berinsfield (Oxfordshire) between about 450 and 550 offer just one example.[151] The uncompromisingly Germanic grave-goods buried with them appeared to provide clear evidence of an immigrant "Anglo-Saxon" community, yet analysis of their teeth showed that fifteen of the nineteen were local people; of the four outsiders, three had probably moved to Oxfordshire from elsewhere in Britain, and only one was certainly a European immigrant, perhaps from south-west Germany rather than the north German plains from which the "Anglo-Saxons" are supposed to have arrived. The Berinsfield community seems to have been largely composed of late Romano-British people who rapidly adopted day-to-day artifacts made in new forms, materials, and styles. Like those buried in other communities, the graves of locally and foreign-born individuals are indistinguishable in their location in the cemetery, in the orientation of their graves, whether they were cremated or buried, or in the goods buried with them. Similar results from elsewhere support the growing consensus that isotopic evidence is "inconsistent with simple models of mass invasion, elite takeover or acculturation."[152] Those results, the impossibility of mapping the cultural origins of grave-goods, the impossibility of distinguishing between supposedly "Anglo-Saxon" and "Late British" communities, and the mixed cultural origins of many fifth- and sixth-century artifactual forms provide little support for the proposition of distinctive Germanic cultures or communities in late antique England.[153]

The consequence is that there must be growing doubt about conventional beliefs regarding the character and importance of post-Roman immigration into Britain: specifically, that it can be assumed largely to have originated in north-west Europe, to have been numerically significant, was characterized by a specific cultural identity, and to have had a formative impact on local communities.

Language

The most lasting achievement attributed to fifth- and sixth-century migrants from north-west Europe is the emergence of English, the language that is believed to have developed from the Germanic languages that they spoke.[154] As we have seen, the term describing both language and people appears, like Athene from the brow of Zeus, to have sprung fully grown into national use by the mid sixth century when the Byzantine historian Procopius mentioned the *Angli*, the English, as one of the three groups that inhabited Britain: the others he listed were the *Brittones* (a term usually applied to everyone living in the island of Britain), and the *Frisiones*;[155] and the term was repeated in the late sixth century by Pope Gregory when he discussed in his letters the conversion of the *Angli* (as opposed to the Picts or Scots) to Christianity.[156] That this was more than fancy on his part is demonstrated by the use of English to record the law code of King Æthelberht of Kent in about 600.[157] Why were the laws recorded in the vernacular rather than in Latin? The answer may lie in royal charters granting vast estates to the endowment of seventh- and eighth-century religious houses, the detail of whose boundaries—the rivers, hedges, and fields that they followed, the trees, fords, and stones that marked them—were recorded in Old English. Geary has argued that this was so that the bounds could be understood and collectively ratified by the English-speaking freemen who came to witness the grant.[158] Since Æthelberht's law code is widely regarded as recording much that was existing customary law, requiring the consent of the men of Kent, the choice of recording it in Old English suggests that the language was already the principal vernacular, in his kingdom at least, by the late sixth century.

How did that happen? The process is opaque. Those who arrived spoke different languages and came in England in small numbers over at least two centuries. They cannot collectively have imposed English on the existing late antique population and Hall has observed that that model "is entirely insufficient to explain the spread of English following the collapse of Roman rule in the region."[159] In response to those difficulties, scholars have adopted the model of elite replacement, arguing that the immigrants rapidly assumed political leadership of communities and territories in the areas in which they settled and that late Romano-Britons adopted Old English in order to achieve recognition and acceptance among that new Germanic aristocracy (see pp. 75–78, below).[160] The second-language status of Brittonic is held to explain the distinctive influence it appears to have had on English syntax.[161] Old English was first learned by adults whose native tongue was British Celtic; they transmitted it imperfectly to their children, who gradually adopted English as their native language, and those mistakes became embedded.[162] The relative paucity of Celtic loanwords in English is explained in terms of the low status to which it is believed Brittonic was relegated. This conclusion may be revised, though, since recent research suggests that Brittonic place-names survived, or were incorporated into Old English place-names, more often than has previously been recognized.[163]

That explanation, and the elite replacement model itself, is problematic for at least two reasons. The first is that the use of English (or any other language) as a second language does not necessarily imply immigration, conquest, or elite domination. Currently about 1.5 billion people across the world speak English, of whom over one billion speak it as a second language. They include seventy-two percent of the population of the Netherlands, seventy-one percent of those in Denmark and seventy percent of those in Sweden, even though this does not the result from their conquest by Britain, from mass migration into these countries by English speakers, or from the domination of their elites by individuals of English origin.[164]

The second is in the assumption that late Romano-British communities were monolingual, predominantly speaking British Celtic.[165] Hall, however, has argued that, at least in lowland England, bi- or multi-lingualism in British Celtic, Late Spoken Latin, and/or Old English was widespread and may account for the unusually close relationship between English syntax and that of the Romance languages.[166] Many place-names, for instance, continued to be referred to by their Latin names alongside the Old English names into which they were often transliterated—Verulamium, for instance, became *Uerlamacaestir*; there were, similarly, Celtic and Old English names in use at the same time for the same place.[167] This is not unusual. There are modern examples of the same phenomenon: Louvain (Belgium), for instance, is the French name for the place that Flemish speakers call Leuven. Little is known about the languages spoken in Britain by the late fourth century. The ancestor of British Celtic was certainly among them but so, too, was a vernacular form of Latin (Late Spoken Latin) that emerged during the period of the Roman occupation of Britain alongside the classical Latin that was the language of imperial administration, learning, and the Roman church. By the early eighth century Bede not only listed the five languages spoken across England—English, Latin (both the classical of the church and learning, and a vernacular form called Late Spoken Latin), British Celtic, Irish, and Pictish; he also assumed some level of bi-/multi-lingualism and noted that most people could speak vernacular Latin.[168]

The larger-scale survival of Latin compared with Celtic elements in lowland English place-names bears Bede's evidence out, suggesting that Late Spoken Latin was at least as commonly, if not more often, spoken than Brittonic in the late antique and early medieval lowlands (Figure 2).[169] There are more Latin loanwords in English than from any other source, many already in use from the earliest period in which the language was developing, and its influence on British Celtic is well known.[170] The widespread distribution of place-names with Latin elements or Old English using Latin loanwords across central and eastern England is striking (indicating, too, that Romano-British institutions and local administration persisted—whether in their original or in evolved forms—into the eighth century at least);[171] and inscriptions in Latin, using imperial formulations, continued to be made in stone into the sixth and seventh centuries—most commonly in the west, where stone is plentiful, but occasionally, too, in the east.[172] There must be a possibility that the principal language of late antique England was not Brittonic but Late Spoken Latin and, in that case, that the emergence of Old English may not necessarily reflect the oppression of Brittonic speakers.

What other explanations are there for the emergence and growing dominance of Old English? Peter Schrijver has proposed that a Germanic dialect that had evolved from trading connections across the North Sea may already have been spoken in England by the fifth century.[173] More controversial is the suggestion that "a non-Latin, non-Brittonic, but possibly West Germanic language" may already have been spoken in eastern Britain during the late Iron Age, five or more centuries earlier.[174] Neither of these propositions may stand the test of time. Their utility lies in their implication that language, migration, and ethnicity are not necessarily linked—a proposition returned to in Chapter 3.

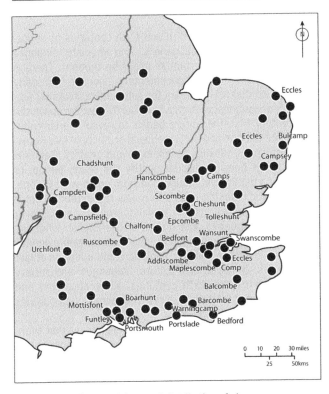

Figure 2. The widespread distribution of place-names
including Latin elements or Latin loanwords across central
and eastern England suggests that the principal post-imperial
language of these regions was Late Spoken Latin
(© Susan Oosthuizen 2018. Sources: Gelling, *Signposts to
the Past*, at p. 85, and Halogen Geospatial Search Facility,
www.halogen.le.ac.uk).

Conclusions

What we know about the fifth and sixth centuries from documentary, archaeological, genetic, and linguistic evidence may not, then, be as certain as might be thought. There is no reliable, contemporary documentary evidence from early British or continental scholars for substantive invasion, settlement, or conquest of Britain from north-west Europe in the fifth century. Material culture begins to reveal the contribution to late antique and early medieval artifacts of late Romano-British craftsmanship, technology, and artistry. Genomic research has been unable to identify the scale, period, or volume of a distinctive immigration from north-west Europe. And linguistic research begins to reveal the extent to which most people in the English lowlands could speak two or even three languages. The origins of the English language itself remain controversial. In all, the most certain evidence appears to show the stability, evolution, and adaption of late Romano-British institutions, culture, languages, and society across the fifth and sixth centuries, while absorbing and evolving in response to influences from across the countries that bordered the North Sea.

Yet, though many modern researchers accept that there are problems with the reliability of the documentary evidence, discuss the scale of the *adventus* in relatively limited terms, acknowledge the diverse origins of "the Anglo-Saxons," and recognize the continuing influence of Romano-British traditions and languages, much scholarship nonetheless remains based on three premises despite their weaknesses: the first is that the departure of the Roman army and civilian administrators was followed by economic collapse and political instability; the second is that little survived of late Romano-British culture, institutions, or language; and the third is that there was "something special" about the volume, character, and cultural identity of fifth- and sixth-century Germanic immigrants whose movement into Britain they take for granted. Together those premises support the persistence of an explanatory model for the emergence of early medieval from late antique Britain that takes the special characteristics of Germanic ethnicity as its starting point. That view is explored in Chapter 3.

Notes

[44] H. P. R. Finberg, "Anglo-Saxon England to 1042," in *The Agrarian History of England and Wales I, ii, AD 43–1042*, ed. H. P. R. Finberg (Cambridge: Cambridge University Press, 1972), 385–525, at 401.

[45] The lists of early Anglo-Saxon kings and their genealogies are not included here since their reliability is questionable. Critiques of their usefulness as primary sources have been undertaken in, for example, David Dumville, "The West Saxon Genealogical Regnal List and the Chronology of Early Wessex," *Peritia* 4, 21 (1985): 21–66; Higham, *Rome, Britain;* Nicholas Higham, *The English Conquest. Gildas and Britain in the Fifth Century* (Manchester: Manchester University Press, 1994).

[46] Philip Freeman, *The World of Saint Patrick* (Oxford: Oxford Scholarship Online, 2014), http://www.oxfordscholarship.com/view/10.1093/acprof:oso/9780199372584.001.0001/acprof-9780199372584-chapter-1, at 7. See also R. P. C. Hanson, "English Translation of the 'Confession' and the 'Letter to Corotius' of Saint Patrick," *Nottingham Medieval Studies* 15 (1971): 3–26.

[47] Gildas, *The Ruin of Britain and Other Documents*, ed. Michael Winterbottom (Chichester: Phillimore, 1978); see also Andrew Breeze, "Where was Gildas Born?," *Northern History* 45, 2 (2008): 347–50.

[48] Bede, *Ecclesiastical History*.

[49] These and the following biographical details are drawn from Hanson, "English Translation of the 'Confession'," 3–26. See also Freeman, *World of St Patrick*, chap. 1.

[50] Freeman, *World of St. Patrick*, 18.

[51] Freeman, *World of St. Patrick*, 20. Patrick was embarrassed by the standard of his writing in classical Latin; he explained that he had had little schooling and had had to learn another language. Which was his first and his second language? He came from a high status Romanized family, whose names were given in Latin, and he attended school until he was sixteen; it seems almost certain that his first language was vernacular Latin—he explained his lack of familiarity with classical Latin by his lack of schooling; the second language he had had to learn seems most likely to have been Hibernian Celtic, after his kidnapping and sale as a slave in Ireland. See also Higham, *Rome, Britain*, 196.

[52] Freeman, *World of St. Patrick*, 8, my addition; Hanson, "English Translation of the 'Confession'," at 20.

[53] Gildas, *Ruin of Britain*.

[54] Higham, *The English Conquest*, 15.

[55] Higham, *The English Conquest*, chap. 5; Sims-Williams, "Settlement of England," at 15; Yorke, "Anglo-Saxon Origin Legends," at 20n32; Charles-Edwards, *Wales and the Britons*, 43–56, 202–19.

[56] Sims-Williams, "Settlement of England," at 15; Higham, *The English Conquest*.

[57] Sims-Williams, "Settlement of England," at 6.

[58] Gildas, *Ruin of Britain*, 20:1.

[59] Higham, *The English Conquest*, 134–37.

[60] Guy Halsall, *Barbarian Migrations and the Roman West 376–568* (Cambridge: Cambridge University Press, 2007), 522–25.

[61] Gildas, *Ruin of Britain*, 23.

[62] Alex Woolf, "An Interpolation in the Text of Gildas's *De Excidio Britanniae*," *Peritia* 16 (2002): 161–67.

[63] James Harland, "Rethinking Ethnicity and 'Otherness' in Early Anglo-Saxon England," *Medieval Histories* 5 (2017): 113–42, at 121–22.

[64] Harland, "Rethinking Ethnicity," at 124–25.

[65] Gildas, *Ruin of Britain*, 23:5; Adolf Berger, ed., *Encyclopedic Dictionary of Roman Law* (Philadelphia: American Philosophical Society, 1953, reprinted 1991), 489, 363.

[66] Gildas, *Ruin of Britain*, 23–24 and 25:2.

[67] Gildas, *Ruin of Britain*, 14, 16, 19, 20:2–3.

[68] Gildas, *Ruin of Britain*, 26:2.

[69] *Gildas, Ruin of Britain*: on judicial structure, 27; productive landscape 3:2–3; prosperity 21:2. For ecclesiastical hierarchy, 66–110; further detail on ecclesiastical organization can be found in Gildas. "Fragments of Lost Letters," in *The Ruin of Britain and Other Documents*, ed. Michael Winterbottom (Chichester: Phillimore, 1978), 80–82, and "The Pentitential of Gildas," in *The Ruin of Britain and Other Documents*, ed. Michael Winterbottom (Chichester: Phillimore, 1978), 84–86. See also John Richardson, "Roman Law in the Provinces," in *The Cambridge Companion to Roman Law*, ed. David Johnson (Cambridge: Cambridge University Press, 2015), 45–58.

[70] Gildas, *Ruin of Britain*: on kings and kingdoms, 25:3, 27–36; deserted towns, 26:2; Harland, "Rethinking Ethnicity," at 125.

[71] Bede, *Ecclesiastical History*.

[72] Sims-Williams, "Settlement of England," at 21; see also Maria Miller, "Bede's Use of Gildas," *English Historical Review* 90, 355 (1975): 241–61.

[73] Sims-Williams, "Settlement of England," at 31. See also David Dumville, "Sub-Roman Britain: History and Legend," *History* 62, 205 (1977): 173–92; Nicholas Higham, *An English Empire. Bede and the Early Anglo-Saxon Kings* (Manchester: Manchester University Press, 1995).

[74] J. McClure, "Bede's Old Testament Kings," in *Ideal and Reality in Frankish and Anglo-Saxon Society*, ed. Patrick Wormald (Oxford: Blackwell, 1983), 76–88; Higham, *An English Empire*, 11–16.

[75] Alaric Hall, "*A Gente Anglorum Appellatur*: The Evidence of Bede's *Historia Ecclesiastica Gentis Anglorum* for the Replacement of Roman Names by English Ones During the Early Anglo-Saxon Period," in *Words in Dictionaries and History: Essays in Honour of R. W. McConchie*, ed. Olga Timofeeva and Tanja Saïly (Amsterdam: Benjamins, 2011), 219–31; Alaric Hall, "Interlinguistic Communication in Bede's *Historia Ecclesiastica Gentis Anglorum*," in *Interfaces Between Language and Culture in Medieval England*, ed. Alaric Hall, Agnes Kiricsci, and Olga Timofeeva, with Bethany Fox (Leiden: Brill, 2010), 37–80.

[76] Higham, *Rome, Britain*, 216.

[77] Susan Oosthuizen, *Tradition and Transformation in Anglo-Saxon England: Archaeology, Common Rights and Landscape* (London: Bloomsbury Academic, 2013), 110–20; see also Katie Hemer, Jane Evans, Carolyn Chenery, and Angela Lamb, "Evidence of Early Medieval Trade and Migration between Wales and the Mediterranean Sea Region," *Journal of Archaeological Science* 40 (2013): 2352–59.

[78] Sue Harrington and Martin Welch, *The Early Anglo-Saxon Kingdoms of Southern Britain AD 450–650: Beneath the Tribal Hidage* (Oxford: Windgather, 2014), 8, my emphasis.

[79] For example, S. B. Leslie, G. Winney, D. Hellenthal, et al., "The Fine-Scale Genetic Structure of the British Population," *Nature* 51 (2015): 309–14.

[80] See, for example, David Dumville, "Kingship, Genealogies and Regnal Lists," in *Early Medieval Kingship*, ed. Peter Sawyer and Ian Wood (Leeds: University of Leeds, 1977), 72–104; Geary, *Myth of Nations*; Higham, *The English Conquest*; Higham, *An English Empire*; Dumville, "West Saxon Genealogical Regnal List."

[81] Sims-Williams, "Settlement of England," at 4, my additions. Sims-Williams offers an extensive and convincing critical discussion of the reliability of the Anglo-Saxon Chronicle on 26–41 of the same paper, concluding (34), that its chronology "is both extremely suspicious and incapable of correction." Evidence from the Chronicle has not been included here.

[82] Stanley Ireland, *Roman Britain: A Sourcebook* (London: Routledge, 2008).

[83] Zosimus, *New History*, ed. Ronald T. Ridley (Leiden: Brill, 1982), bk. 6, 5; Michael Kulikowski, "Barbarians in Gaul, Usurpers in Britain," *Britannia* 31 (2000): 325–45, at 332–33.

[84] Zosimus, *New History*, bk. 6, 10.

[85] Cited in Philip Bartholomew, "Fifth-Century Facts," *Britannia* 13 (1982): 261–70, at 261, 263n10.

[86] Bartholomew, "Fifth-Century Facts," at 263–64.

[87] Zosimus, *New History*, bk. 6, 10; Bartholomew, "Fifth-Century Facts," at 261. Olympiodorus's text has not survived, but is believed to have been reliably reproduced in histories written by three scholars, each largely based in Constantinople: Philostorgius, ca. 440; Sozomen, ca. 443; and Zosimus, ca. 498–502—see J. F. Matthews, "Olympiodorus of Thebes and the History of the West (A.D. 407–425)," *Journal of Roman Studies* 60, 1 (1970): 79–97, at 80–82.

[88] Bartholomew, "Fifth-Century Facts," at 262–63.

[89] Bartholomew, "Fifth-Century Facts," at 262.

[90] Bartholomew, "Fifth-Century Facts," at 263.

[91] OL.CCXCVII.XVI, in Richard Burgess, "The Gallic Chronicle of 452: A New Critical Edition with a Brief Introduction," *Society and Culture in Late Antique Gaul: Revisiting the Sources*, ed. Ralph Mathisen and Danuta Shanzer (London: Routledge, 2001), 52–83. Bartholomew, "Fifth-Century Facts," at 263–65, my addition; Maria Miller, "The Last British Entry in the 'Gallic Chronicles'," *Britannia* 9 (1978): 315–18, at 317.

[92] OL.CCCVI.XVIII, in Burgess, "The Gallic Chronicle"; the disputed entry for 441/2 reads "*Britanniae usque ad hoc tempus uariis cladibus eventibusque laceratae in ditionem Saxonum rediguntur.*" For a slightly different reading see *Chronica Minora Saec. IV. V. VI. VII*, ed. Theodor Mommsen, 3 vols., *Monumenta Germaniae Historica Scriptores: Auctores Antiquissimi*, 9 (Berlin: Weidmann, 1892), 1:660. Bartholomew ("Fifth-Century Facts," 279) includes this under 445/6; I have followed Mommsen in using 441/2.

[93] Miller, "The Last British Entry," at 315; Bartholomew, "Fifth-Century Facts," at 269–70.

[94] R. W. Burgess, "The Dark Ages Return to Fifth-Century Britain: The 'Restored' Gallic Chronicle' Exploded," *Britannia* 21 (1990): 185–95; see also R. W. Burgess, "The Gallic Chronicle," *Britannia* 25 (1994): 240–43.

[95] Steven Muhlberger, "The Gallic Chronicle of 452 and its

Authority for British Events," *Britannia* 14 (1983): 23–33; Michael Jones and John Casey, "The Gallic Chronicle Restored: A Chronology for the Anglo-Saxon Invasions and the End of Roman Britain," *Britannia* 19 (1988): 367–98; and Michael Jones and John Casey, "The Gallic Chronicle Exploded?," *Britannia* 22 (1991): 212–15.

[96] Anthony Barrett, "Saint Germanus and the British Missions," *Britannia* 40 (2009): 197–217, at 201, 204. For a similarly positive interpretation of the accuracy of the record, see also Nicholas Higham, "Constantius, St. Germanus and Fifth-Century Britain," *Early Medieval Europe* 22, 2 (2014): 113–37; Constantius of Lyon, *The Life of Saint Germanus of Auxerre*, in *Soldiers of Christ: Saints and Saints' Lives From Late Antiquity and the Early Middle Ages*, ed. Thomas Noble (Philadelphia: Pennsylvania University Press, 1995), 75–106, at chap. 17.

[97] Barrett, "Saint Germanus," at 202.

[98] Barrett, "Saint Germanus," at 204–5; *Life of St. Germanus*, chaps. 14 and 17–18.

[99] Barrett, "Saint Germanus," at 204; *Life of St. Germanus*, chap. 18, refers to Britain as "this most wealthy island" which was "rendered secure in every sense."

[100] Millett, *Romanization*, 185.

[101] Helena Hamerow, "Migration Theory and the Anglo-Saxon 'Identity Crisis'," in *Migrations and Invasions in Archaeological Explanation*, ed. John Chapman and Helena Hamerow (Oxford: Noyes, 1997), 33–44, at 33.

[102] Taylor, *Village and Farmstead*, 64, 83.

[103] For example, Royal Commission on Historical Monuments (England) (RCHM(E)), *An Inventory of Archaeological Sites in Central Northamptonshire* (London: HMSO, 1979), xxxi–xlix; Taylor, *Village and Farmstead*; David Hall, *The Fenland Project, Number 2. Cambridgeshire Survey: Peterborough to March*, EAA, 35 (Colchester: East Anglian Archaeology, 1987); David McOmish, David Field, and Graham Brown, *The Field Archaeology of Salisbury Plain* (Swindon: English Heritage, 2002); Roberts and Wrathmell, *Region and Place*.

[104] Martin, *Cruciform Brooch*, 78.

[105] See, for example, Tom Williamson, "East Anglia's Character and the 'North Sea World'," in *East Anglia and Its North Sea World in the Middle Ages*, ed. David Bates and Robert Liddiard (Woodbridge: Boydell and Brewer, 2013), 44–62; and Martin, *Cruciform Brooch*.

[106] Lloyd Laing, "Romano-British Metalworking and the Anglo-Saxons," in *Britons in Anglo-Saxon England*, ed. Nicholas Higham (Woodbridge: Boydell and Brewer, 2007), 42–56.

[107] For example, Gale Owen-Crocker, "British Wives and Slaves? Romano-British Techniques in 'Women's Work'," in *Britons in Anglo-Saxon England*, ed. Nicholas Higham (Woodbridge: Boydell and Brewer, 2007), 80–90.

[108] Gareth Williams, "The Circulation, Minting and Use of Coins in East Anglia, *c.* A.D. 580–675," in *East Anglia and Its North Sea World in the Middle Ages* (Woodbridge: Boydell and Brewer 2013), 120–36.

[109] Simon Esmonde Cleary, "The Ending(s) of Roman Britain," in *The Oxford Handbook of Anglo-Saxon Archaeology*, ed. David Hinton, Helena Hamerow, and Sally Crawford (Oxford: Oxford University Press, 2011), 13–19.

[110] Williams, "Coins in East Anglia," at 122–25.

[111] Simon Esmonde Cleary, *The Ending of Roman Britain* (London: Routledge, 1991); see also Simon Esmonde Cleary, "The Roman to Medieval Transition," in *Britons and Romans: Advancing an Archaeological Agenda*, ed. Simon James and Martin Millett (York: Council for British Archaeology, 2001), 90–97.

[112] Gerrard, *Ruin of Roman Britain*, 100.

[113] Gerrard, *Ruin of Roman Britain*, 97–99 and 103.

[114] Gerrard, *Ruin of Roman Britain*, 84–86.

[115] P. A. Tyers, *Atlas of Roman Pottery* (1996, 2014), http://potsherd.net/atlas/Ware/NVCC.html.

[116] Malcolm Lynne, "The End of Roman Pottery Production in Roman Britain," *Internet Archaeology* 41 (2016); Jeremy Evans, "Balancing the Scales: Romano-British Pottery in Early Late Antiquity," *Late Antique Archaeology* 10, 1 (2013): 425–50, at 443.

[117] For example, James Gerrard, ed., "Themed Issue: Romano-British Pottery in the Fifth Century," *Internet Archaeology* 41 (2016); Kevin Fitzpatrick-Matthews, "The Perils of Periodization: Roman Ceramics in Britain after 400 CE," *Fragments* 5 (2016): 1–33. See also the summary of recent work on Lincoln in Caitlin Green, "Romano-British Pottery in the Fifth- to Sixth-Century Lincoln Region," June 12, 2016, http://www.caitlingreen.org/2016/06/romano-british-pottery-fifth-century-lincoln.html#fn5.

[118] Peter Murphy, "The Anglo-Saxon Landscape and Rural Economy: Some Results from Sites in East Anglia and Essex," in *Environment and Economy in Anglo-Saxon England*, ed. James Rackham, CBA Research Report, 89 (York: Council for British Archaeology, 1994), 25–37, at 25–27, 37; Petra Dark, *The Environment of Britain in the First Millennium A.D.* (London: Duckworth, 2000), chap. 5; Glenn Foard, "Medieval Woodland, Agriculture and Industry in Rocking-

ham Forest, Northamptonshire," *Medieval Archaeology* 45 (2001): 41–95; G. Hey, *Yarnton: Saxon and Medieval Settlement and Landscape* (Oxford: Oxbow, 2004), 40–41; David Miles, *Archaeology at Barton Court Farm, Abingdon, Oxon.* (Oxford: Oxford Archaeological Unit, 1984), 25; Oliver Rackham, *History of the Countryside* (London: Dent, 1986), 67.

[119] See note 188, above, and also Martin Carver, *The Birth of a Borough: An Archaeological Study of Anglo-Saxon Stafford* (Woodbridge: Boydell and Brewer, 2010), 59, 65; Hey, *Yarnton*, 40–41; Stephen Upex, "Landscape Continuity and Fossilisation of Roman Fields," *Archaeological Journal* 159 (2002): 77–108, at 89; Murphy, "Anglo-Saxon Landscape and Rural Economy," at 37; Andrew Rogerson, Alan Davison, David Pritchard, and Robert Silvester, *Barton Bendish and Caldecote: Fieldwork in South-West Norfolk*, EAA, 80 (Colchester: East Anglian Archaeology, 1997), 20, 23; Andrew Lawson, *The Archaeology of Witton, near North Walsham, Norfolk*, EAA, 18 (Colchester: East Anglian Archaeology, 1983), 75; Alan Davison, *The Evolution of Settlement in Three Parishes in South-East Norfolk*, EAA, 49 (Colchester: East Anglian Archaeology, 1990), 18–19; Della Hooke, *Trees in Anglo-Saxon England: Literature, Lore and Landscape* (Woodbridge: Boydell and Brewer, 2011), 31; Peter Hayes and Tom Lane, *The Fenland Project, Number 5: Lincolnshire Survey, the South-West Fens*, EAA, 55 (Colchester: East Anglian Archaeology, 1992), 213, 253; Pam Crabtree, "Agricultural Innovation and Socio-Economic Change in Early Medieval Europe: Evidence from Britain and France," *World Archaeology* 42, 1 (2010): 122–36, at 124; Susan Oosthuizen, *The Anglo-Saxon Fenland* (Oxford: Windgather, 2017), 90–96.

[120] David Klingle, *The Use of Skeletal Evidence to Understand the Transition from Roman to Anglo-Saxon Cambridgeshire and Bedfordshire*, BAR British Series, 569 (Oxford: British Archaeological Reports, 2012), 211–13.

[121] Gerrard, *Ruin of Roman Britain*, 258; see Esmonde Cleary, *Ending of Roman Britain*, chap. 4, especially at 113–14 for a contrasting view.

[122] See notes 118 and 119 above.

[123] Gerrard, *Ruin of Roman Britain*, 165, 239, 255–57.

[124] For example, Esmonde Cleary, *Ending of Roman Britain*, 123–29.

[125] For example, Gavin Speed, *Towns in the Dark. Urban Transformations from Late Roman Britain to Anglo-Saxon England* (Oxford: Archaeopress Archaeology, 2014), 136–41; for a critical review of this volume by James Gerrard, see *Britannia* 46 (2015): 442. See

also Allen Lane, "Wroxeter and the End of Roman Britain," *Antiquity* 88 (2014): 501–15.

[126] Maria Medlycott, *The Roman Town of Great Chesterford*, EAA, 137 (Colchester: East Anglian Archaeology, 2011); Steven Bassett, "In Search of the Origins of the Anglo-Saxon Kingdoms," in *The Origins of the Anglo-Saxon Kingdoms,* ed. Steven Bassett (Leicester: Leicester University Press, 1989), 3–27; Jeremy Haslam, "The Development and Topography of Saxon Cambridge," *Proceedings of the Cambridge Antiquarian Society* 72 (1984): 13–29.

[127] Chris Loveluck and Lloyd Laing, "Britons and Anglo-Saxons," in *The Oxford Handbook of Anglo-Saxon Archaeology*, ed. David Hinton, Helena Hamerow, and Sally Crawford (Oxford: Oxford University Press, 2011), 534–55, at 537.

[128] Thomas Green, *Britons and Anglo-Saxons: Lincolnshire AD 400–650* (Lincoln: History of Lincolnshire Committee, 2012).

[129] Bede, *Ecclesiastical History*, bk. 4, chap. 19.

[130] P. H. Reaney, *Place-Names of Cambridgeshire and the Isle of Ely* (Cambridge: Cambridge University Press, 1943), 75–78; John Baker, "OE sæte and sætan Place-names," *Journal of the English Place-Name Society* 46 (2015): 45–81.

[131] Rob Collins, "Soldiers to Warriors: The Roman Frontier in the Fifth Century," in *Late Roman Silver: the Trapain Treasure in Context*, ed. Fraser Hunter and Kenneth Painter (Edinburgh: Society of Antiquaries of Scotland, 2013), 29–43, at 31.

[132] Collins, "Soldiers to Warriors," at 32–40.

[133] For example, Hemer, Evans, Chenery, et al., "Evidence of Early Medieval Trade and Migration"; Hella Eckhardt, Gundula Müldner, and Mary Lewis, "People on the Move in Roman Britain," *World Archaeology* 46, 4 (2014): 534–50; Leslie, et al., "The Fine-Scale Genetic Structure"; Lara Cassidy, Rui Martiniano, Eileen Murphy, Matthew Teasdale, James Mallory, Barrie Hartwell, and Daniel Bradley, "Neolithic and Bronze Age Migration to Ireland and the Establishment of the Insular Atlantic Genome," *Proceedings of the National Academy of the Sciences of the United States of America*, 113, 2 (2016): 368–73.

[134] For nuanced views of population movement, see Catherine Hills, "The Anglo-Saxon Migration to Britain: An Archaeological Perspective," *Tagungen des Landesmuseums für Vorgeschichte Halle* 20 (2017): 1–15; and (for a wider-ranging discussion), Guy Halsall, "Two Worlds Become One: A 'Counter-Intuitive' View of the Roman Army and 'Germanic' Migration," *German History* 32, 4 (2014): 515–32.

[135] Susan Reynolds, "Medieval *Origines Gentium* and the Com-

munity of the Realm," *History* 68 (1983): 375–90, at 379 (my emphasis).

[136] M. Weale, D. Weiss, R. Jager, N. Bradman, and M. Thomas, "Y Chromosome Evidence for Anglo-Saxon Mass Migration," *Molecular Biological Evolution* 19 (2002): 1008–21; C. Capelli, N. Redhead, J. Abernathy, et al., "A Y-chromosome Census of the British Isles," *Current Biology* 13 (2003): 979–84; Leslie, et al., "The Fine-Scale Genetic Structure," at 310, 313–14; see also S. Hughes, Andrew Millard, Sam Lucy, et al., "Anglo-Saxon Origins Investigated by Isotopic Analysis of Burials from Berinsfield, Oxfordshire, UK," *Journal of Archaeological Science* 42 (2014): 81–92.

[137] Leslie, et al., "The Fine-Scale Genetic Structure," at 310, 313–14.

[138] Leslie, et al., "The Fine-Scale Genetic Structure," at 313; Stephan Schiffels, Wolfgang Haak, Pirita Paajanen, et al., "Iron Age and Anglo-Saxon Genomes from East England Reveal British Migration History," *Nature Communications* 10408 (2016): 1–9.

[139] Leslie, et al., "The Fine-Scale Genetic Structure," at Figure 2, 311; Methods, Figure 6.

[140] Leslie, et al., "The Fine-Scale Genetic Structure," Methods.

[141] Leslie, et al., "The Fine-Scale Genetic Structure," Extended Data Figure 9. The assumptions underpinning the tortuous explanations adopted to explain this result in such a way that it might still be held to record the settlement are explored in Chapter 3.

[142] Jane Kershaw and Ellen Røyrvik, "The 'People of the British Isles' Project and Viking Settlement in England," *Antiquity* 90, 354 (2016): 1670–80.

[143] Patrick Geary and Krishna Veeramah, "Mapping European Population Movement through Genomic Research," *Medieval Worlds* 4 (2016): 65–78.

[144] Geary and Veeramah, "Mapping European Population," 69.

[145] Geary and Veeramah, "Mapping European Population," 70.

[146] Schiffels, et al., "Iron Age and Anglo-Saxon Genomes", Table 1.

[147] Schiffels, et al., "Iron Age and Anglo-Saxon Genomes", 7.

[148] Schiffels, et al., "Iron Age and Anglo-Saxon Genomes", 7.

[149] Gerrard, *Ruin of Roman Britain*, 18.

[150] See also note 231 below. For example, Paul Budd, Andrew Millard, Carolyn Chenery, et al., "Investigating Population Movement by Stable Isotope Analysis: A Report from Britain," *Antiquity* 78, 299 (2004): 127–41; J. Montgomery, Jane Evans, Dominic Powlesland, and A. Roberts, "Continuity or Colonization in Anglo-Saxon England? Isotope Evidence for Mobility, Subsistence Practice, and Status at

West Heslerton," *American Journal of Physical Anthropology* 126 (2005): 123–38; Sam Lucy, Richard Newman, Natasha Dodwell, et al., "The Burial of a Princess? The Later Seventh-Century Cemetery at Westfield Farm, Ely," *Antiquaries Journal* 89 (2009): 81–141; Jane Evans, Carole Chenery, and J. Montgomery, "Summary of Strontium and Oxygen Isotope Variation in Archaeological Tooth Enamel Excavated from Britain," *Journal of the Analysis of Atomic Spectrometry* 27 (2012): 754–64; S. E. Groves, C. A. Roberts, Sam Lucy, et al., "Mobility Histories of 7th–9th century AD People Buried at Early Medieval Bamburgh, Northumberland," *American Journal of Physical Anthropology* 151 (2012): 462–76.

[151] Hughes, Millard, Lucy, et al., "Anglo-Saxon Origins," at 90.

[152] Susan Hughes, Andrew Millard, Carolyn Chenery, Geoff Nowell, and D. Pearson, "Isotopic Analysis of Burials from the Early Anglo-Saxon Cemetery at Eastbourne, Sussex," *Journal of Archaeological Science* 19 (2018): 513–25, at 513; Sam Lucy and Andrew Reynolds, "Burial in Early Medieval England and Wales: Past, Present and Future," in *Burial in Early Medieval England and Wales*, ed. Sam Lucy and Andrew Reynolds (London: Society for Medieval Archaeology, 2002), 1–23, at 10.

[153] See, for example, Stefan Brather, "Acculturation and Ethnogenesis Along the Frontier: Rome and the Ancient Germans in an Archaeological Perspective," in *Borders, Barriers and Ethnogenesis*, ed. Florin Curta (Turnhout: Brepols, 2005), 139–72; Howard Williams, "Mortuary Practices in Early Anglo-Saxon England," in *The Oxford Handbook of Anglo-Saxon Archaeology*, ed. David Hinton, Helena Hamerow, and Sally Crawford (Oxford: Oxford University Press, 2011), 238–65.

[154] Hilda Tristram, "Why Don't the English Speak Welsh?," in *Britons in Anglo-Saxon England*, ed. Nicholas Higham (Woodbridge: Boydell and Brewer, 2007), 192–214.

[155] Procopius, *History of the Wars: Books VII and VIII*, VIII.xx.4–8.

[156] Higham, *An English Empire*, 251–53; Bede, *Ecclesiastical History*, bk. 1, chap. 23; *The Earliest Life of Gregory the Great*, chap. 9.

[157] Patrick Wormald, *The First Code of English Law* (Canterbury: Canterbury Commemoration Society, 2005).

[158] Patrick Geary, "Land, Language and Memory in Europe 700–1100," *Transactions of the Royal Historical Society* 9 (1999): 169–84. See also Patrick Wormald, "Charters, Law and the Settlement of Disputes in Anglo-Saxon England," in *The Settlement of Disputes in Early Medieval Europe*, ed. Wendy Davies and Paul

Fouracre (Cambridge: Cambridge University Press, 1986), 149–68, at 161; Patrick Wormald, *Legal Culture in the Early Medieval West: Law as Text, Image and Experience* (London: Hambledon, 1999), 172; Matthew Innes, "Memory, Orality and Literacy in an Early Medieval Society," *Past and Present* 158 (1998): 3–36, at 34.

[159] Hall, "*A Gente Anglorum Appellatur*," at 219.

[160] See, for example, Higham, *Rome, Britain*, 192–208.

[161] Richard Coates, "Invisible Britons: The View from Linguistics," in *Britons in Anglo-Saxon England*, ed. Nicholas Higham (Woodbridge: Boydell and Brewer, 2007), 172–91. For the antiquity of these views, see Maitland, *Domesday Book*, 222.

[162] Tristram, "Why Don't the English Speak Welsh?"

[163] Hall, "*A Gente Anglorum Appellatur*."

[164] World Economic Forum, November 16, 2016, "Which Countries are Best at English as a Second Language?" https://medium.com/world-economic-forum/which-countries-are-best-at-english-as-a-second-language-d4781d077ba6.

[165] For example, Tristram, "Why Don't the English Speak Welsh?"; Philip Durkin, *Borrowed Words: A History of Loanwords in English* (Oxford: Oxford University Press, 2014), at chap. 5.

[166] Hall, "*A gente Anglorum appellatur*"; Hall, "Interlinguistic Communication," at 41–43.

[167] Hall, "Interlinguistic Communication," at 60.

[168] Bede, *Ecclesiastical History*, bk. 1, chap. 1; Hall, "Interlinguistic Communication," at 41–43.

[169] Peter Schrijver, "The Rise and Fall of British Latin: Evidence from English and Brittonic," in *The Celtic Roots of English*, ed. Markku Filppula, Juhani Klemola, and Heli Pitkänen (Joensuu: University of Joensuu, 2002): 87–110.

[170] Durkin, *Borrowed Words*, chap. 6 and at 425–26; Tristram, "Why Don't the English Speak Welsh?," at 197n29; Peter Schrijver, *Language Contact and the Origins of the Germanic Languages* (London: Routledge, 2014), 33–34, 48; Hall, "Interlinguistic Communication," at 41–43.

[171] Margaret Gelling, *Signposts to the Past*: *Place-Names and the History of England* (London: Dent, 1978), Map 2 at 85. Distribution of *ceaster* place-names, halogen.le.ac.uk; see also note 165.

[172] Charles-Edwards, *Wales and the Britons*, 116–73: *Corpus of Anglo-Saxon Stone Sculpture*, Durham University, http://www.ascorpus.ac.uk; David Petts, "Christianity and Cross-Channel Connectivity in Late and Sub-Roman Britain," in *AD 410: The History and Archaeology of Late Roman and Sub-Roman Britain*, ed. Fiona

Haarer and Rob Collins (London: Society for the Promotion of Roman Studies, 2014), 73–88, at 74. Ovin's cross, now in Ely Cathedral, and the Hedda Stone, now in Peterborough Cathedral, offer East Anglian examples.

[173] Schrijver, *Language Contact*, 127–30.

[174] Daphne Nash Briggs, "The Language of Inscriptions on Icenian Coinage," in *The Iron Age in Northern East Anglia: New Work in the Land of the Iceni*, ed. J. A. Davies, BAR British Series, 549 (Oxford: British Archaeological Reports, 2011), 83–102, at 99.

Chapter 3

Ethnicity as an Explanation

Most accounts of late antique and early medieval England take for granted the distinctive and contrasting ethnicities— that is, collective social identities characterized by specific cultural traits—of Germanic immigrant groups and late Romano-British communities. Yet ethnicity is a complex and difficult concept to adduce in historical explanation.[175] It is virtually indefinable since it is socially rather than biologically constructed, offering an implausibly large number of possible variables that are not fixed but change over time.[176] People are not born speaking a particular language, or practising specific social customs.[177] The greater the geographic range of identified with one or another ethnic grouping, the greater the variation is likely to be between the households, communities, and regions of which it is made up. Nor does ethnicity necessarily permeate all aspects of individual or collective identity. It is often invisible and irrelevant. Ethnicity is, more-over, dynamic, evolving, multilayered, and kaleidoscopic, shifting with interaction across innumerable contexts—age, gender, belief, status, and so on—and by social relationship, geography, and stage in life course. Depending on their ages, gender, and status, for example, even people claiming the same ethnicity and living in the same household may speak different dialects, eat dissimilar foods, and have diverse social traditions.[178]

Such problems are exacerbated by the term "Anglo-Saxon" which implicitly assumes a specific ethnicity. As a consequence arguments, interpretations, and models for the period have a tendency to become circular. Many begin by assuming the general reliability of early documentary evidence. Even where it is acknowledged that the details of the *adventus* recorded by Gildas and Bede cannot be relied upon, the historicity of the *adventus* itself is accepted. That presumption frames the interpretation of evidence—already typologized as "Anglo-Saxon"—of artifacts, buildings, fields, burials, and so on of communities which are turned "fully-clothed into the actors mentioned in the historical sources."[179] For example, an archaeologist excavating grave-goods conventionally identified as "early Anglo-Saxon" is likely to interpret the individuals with whom they were buried as "Anglo-Saxons"; subsequent analysis of the distribution of grave-goods among the burials—for example by type of artifact, by gender of the individual, by his/her age—will produce conclusions about the character of a community assumed to be Germanic. A recent study of the emergent Anglo-Saxon kingdom of the South Saxons, for instance, assumes the accuracy of the documentary record of the migrations, and interprets the history of the area in binary terms ranging British populations against Germanic newcomers. Its research questions include "Did the Germanic people take over existing favoured settlement areas" and "Does the distribution of the cemeteries represent the extent of the Anglo-Saxon settlement?"[180] A more neutral phrasing of the first question might be "Was the distribution or internal geography of early medieval settlement influenced by ethnicity?" The last question assumes that the ethnicity of Germanic burials can be identified, that burials within any one cemetery will be restricted to individuals claiming a single ethnic identity, and that "Anglo-Saxon" ethnicity was predicated on descent; that question contains so many implicit expectations that it cannot properly be asked.

Yet the assumption of the cultural distinctiveness of "the Anglo-Saxons" remains the foundation of much of the historiography that explains the presence of Germanic and late Roman material culture along the other English coasts that face Europe as well as further inland.[181] Anglo-Saxon immigrants are said to have established settled communities in Wessex by the end of the fifth century.[182] Typologies of artifacts found in the emergent Anglo-Saxon kingdom of the South Saxons have been interpreted as signatures of Germanic ethnicity, exemplifying Bede's record of the settlement of the region by Saxons and Jutes.[183] Around Lincoln, it is suggested, "the Britons of the country of *Lindēs [were] ... able to physically constrain the immigrants into the region" for a considerable time from the mid-fifth century onwards.[184] The progress of the Saxon advance was regarded as irresistible in the west;[185] and in Deira in the north, despite strong evidence for the assimilation of Germanic migrants within existing British communities, research has concluded that "an 'English' supremacy and identity were adopted relatively quickly at the expense of British freedoms, and in the face of British resistance."[186]

The initial settlement of 'the Anglo-Saxons" in East Anglia remains a dominant theme in archaeological interpretation, too. Specific forms of brooch found across eastern England, for instance, have been interpreted as an index for settler communities whose origins lay in "the Anglian homelands, north of the Elbe in Germany."[187] Finds of Scandinavian wrist clasps have also been identified with Bede's Angles and, it is contended, implied a revolutionary, imported change in forms of women's dress. The argument is based on the premise that, because "costume, and especially female costume, is commonly a strong identity-bearing aspect of material culture," it therefore reflected an immigrant ethnicity.[188] The correlation of styles of artifact with the details of their manufacture and the specificities of their use could thus be used to infer population movement into the region from southern Scandinavia.[189]

The flaw in those arguments is, of course, that while imported artifacts may well have been statements of identity, that identity was not necessarily correlated with an immigrant ethnicity. They may instead simply have been adopted, whether in whole or in part, as an expression of popular fashion and may have arrived in Britain in any number of ways other than as the possessions of immigrants using them to signify their ethnicity. Henig, for instance, has argued that the designs of and motifs on fifth- to seventh-century belt-buckles and flat circular brooches, made in England by late antique craftsmen and often attributed to "early Anglo-Saxon" innovation, are derived from late Roman signifiers of prestige.[190] As he says, the nationality of those who made them or of those who wore them is as unknown as how they were then perceived, and "whether their taste was 'Germanic' lies in the beholder's eye."[191] It is worth remembering Benedict Biscop, the seventh-century abbot of Wearmouth, too, just one of many who travelled extensively between Britain and the continent in that period. He made at least five such journeys, of which four were to Rome. Rather like those who undertook the Grand Tour a millennium later, albeit with ecclesiastical rather than secular motives, he brought back with him all he thought necessary to recreate in Wearmouth the architecture, furnishings, and liturgy of the Roman church: books, vestments, relics, paintings, and "sacred vessels," as well as masons "to build him a church in the Roman style," glaziers to make glass for its windows and lanterns, and a chanter to teach his monks the "Roman mode of chanting, singing and ministering."[192] The material culture that expressed his religious identity was not that of his origins and upbringing—he was a Northumbrian, not a Roman, nobleman; he was born in Britain, not in the Mediterranean.

A present-day example—necessarily imperfect—illustrates the problem of linking material culture with immigration and colonization. The map underlying Figure 3 demonstrates how the North Sea and the rivers that flow into it form a region encouraging waterborne contact between Scandinavia, Germany, Denmark, and the Low Countries.[193] The dots represent the locations of IKEA stores in England in 2018. Let us imagine that in (say) two thousand years' time all documentary evidence from the twenty-first century had disappeared and that only archaeological evidence for the stores survived together with distributions of their goods that

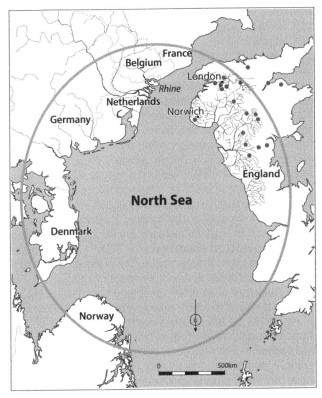

Figure 3. The distribution of IKEA stores in England in 2018 highlights flaws in the assumption that fifth- and sixth-century material culture is inevitably an assertion of immigrant ethnicities. (© Susan Oosthuizen 2018. Sources: Base map: Williamson, "East Anglia's character and the 'North Sea World'," p. 45; www.ikea.co.uk).

diminished in volume with distance from the store. Archaeologists would be likely to note IKEA's considerable stylistic influence on modern British furniture design. They might interpret the evidence as that of the colonization of Britain by Sweden during the late twentieth and early twenty-first centuries and the stores as central places designed to state and preserve the immigrants' Swedish identity. We, however, know that the distribution of the stores is evidence of trade rather than colonization, and that the distribution of their goods reflects the popularity of Swedish design in British homes. There is no link with Swedish ethnicity in Britain. Similarly, if Swedish individuals in England were identified in the forty-first century from isotopic evidence it would be a false inference to argue that their presence was linked to the distribution of IKEA's goods. Only a small minority of the hundred thousand Swedes living in London in 2018, for instance, are likely to have arrived as a consequence of employment by IKEA.[194] Almost all are likely to have come independently. The presence of Swedish artifacts and individuals is not evidence of colonization nor of the statement of an ethnic identity in twenty-first-century Britain. This is not to argue, returning to our own period, that all arguments are false that assume that the presence of Germanic or Scandinavian goods in late antique and early medieval England are the evidence of migration and the retention by those immigrants of an identity based on ethnicity. It is to argue that other explanations beyond migration and colonization are possible and also need attention.

A number of scholars have pointed to the possibility of unwarranted bias in historical explanations based on ethnicity for explaining change in post-Roman Britain.[195] This is because the question that logically follows the premise of an distinctive "Anglo-Saxon" identity in the origins of the English is, "What were the cultural traits that fitted Germanic immigrants better for power, wealth and status than those of the Romano-British elite whom they are supposed to have replaced?" Goffart, for instance, has decried the emphasis on the "Germanness of the migrations" noting that it resonates with the history of nineteenth-century British and twentieth-century German expansionism.[196] Sociologists have described models that foreground ethnicity as ethnic-absolutism, a "fairly static view of ethnicity as more crucial to one's identity than other social categories," calling for the explicit justification of this approach if it is chosen as an explanatory model.[197] Others have made similar criticisms, pointing out the teleological application of modern notions of nationality to early medieval notions of identity.[198] Susan Reynolds has lucidly pointed out the fundamental misconception on which the extrapolation of such stereotypes from documentary evidence, material culture and language is based: "It is not merely morally repugnant in so far as it has been connected with ideas of a hierarchy of races: it is intellectually defective because it implies that cultural and political communities are in reality and in essence also communities of biological descent."[199]

The unarticulated assumption of an "Anglo-Saxon" ethnicity is based on three braided premises: that the cultural traditions of Romano-Britons and "Anglo-Saxons" could be, and were, distinguished by their respective communities at the time; that the latter seized social and political ascendancy over the former; and that the newcomers were able achieve that dominance because their cultural characteristics, their ethnicity, fitted them better for leadership than did those of their opponents.[200] The remainder of this chapter examines each of those assumptions in turn.

The Problem of Cultural Stereotypes

Were there distinctive "Romano-British" and "Anglo-Saxon" cultural traditions, and were they distinguished by their respective late antique or early medieval communities? Historiographical interpretations frequently assume a positive answer to both questions and they are frequently framed in terms of cultural stereotypes. The difficulty with such characterizations is that they tend to be based on extended inferences drawn from evidence for which other interpretations are possible (see Chapter 4).

On the one hand, late Romano-British civilian governance, both local and regional, tends to be described in terms of its relative weakness and its consequent inability to withstand a Germanic advance. The inadequacies of that leadership tend to be characterized by a reluctance to accept and adapt to the changes implicit in the new post-Roman order. Once the *adventus* had begun, the inference is frequently made that the late Romano-British elite simply had as little to do with the newcomers as possible.[201]

The contrapuntal political, military, and social success of the immigrants tends similarly to be premised on their ethnicity. Wilson, for example, described "the clear distinction of material culture and political organization between the Anglo-Saxons and the Romano-British population of England ... The Anglo-Saxons came from a Germanic stock."[202] A quarter of a century later Ward-Perkins explained that "the Germanic invaders absorbed very little of the native culture of Britain," choosing to maintain "a strong sense of difference."[203] Some are portrayed as young men, arriving in small groups and prepared to achieve status and wealth by violence, whether as individuals or by banding together with others of similar origin. Some are described as raiders who settled where they had once plundered, perhaps of peasant rather than elite background. Entrepreneurial in outlook, they were able to seize existing kingdoms or territories, or establish new ones, employing or enslaving late Romano-British populations in the process. In some cases that rapid assumption of power and leadership may have reflected, at least in part, already established habits of lordship. The wealth and status of those migrants and their descendants may have given them a reproductive advantage compared with impoverished, lower status, late Romano-British communities. As a consequence, the latter increasingly began to adopt a Germanic ethnicity—expressed in both language and material culture—to better their life chances.[204]

There are difficulties in using cultural stereotyping of both Romano-British and Anglo-Saxon in explaining change over time when there is so little evidence to support it. The principal objection becomes apparent if one experiments, for instance, by replacing "Romano-British," "Germanic," or "Anglo-Saxon" in such narratives with the names of other, more modern, disadvantaged, or colonizing groups. The characterization of entire communities as (say) inadequate or natural leaders remains an unacceptable method of historical enquiry even if the people to whom it is applied are dead—in the same way that Auden explained that it is dishonourable to read other people's letters while they are out of the room even if they only absent because they have died.[205] What, then, is the evidence for the significance of ethnicity in late antique Britain?

Interrogating the Evidence for the Significance of Ethnicity

Four sources are conventionally adduced for the existence of distinctive "Romano-British" and "Anglo-Saxon" cultural traditions, and their recognition in late antique or early medieval England:

- References to -*wealh* (individuals identified in some way or another with late Romano-British tradition) and *englisc* in the late seventh-century laws of king Ine of Wessex;
- Allusions to *gens, nationes*, and *populi* in the writings of Gildas and Bede;
- Linguistic analyses of the relationship between Brittonic (British Celtic) and Old English;
- Interpretations of genomic data.

Each is examined in turn below.

The Laws of King Ine of Wessex

The earliest surviving documentary references to -*wealh* occur in the late seventh-century laws of King Ine of Wessex, drawn up ca. 688–ca. 693. It is one of only four surviving seventh-century law codes.[206] All are considered to have been based on and to include long-standing, possibly Romano-British, customary law.[207]

Historians have tended to assume that the naming of -*wealh* in Ine's laws was evidence of an awareness of ethnic distinctions in late seventh-century England, and were intended to signal differences between them and *engliscne*, to whom the rest of the code referred. Ward-Perkins, for instance, referred to the "binary ethnic distinction that appears in Ine's law";[208] Grimmer assumed that "there was a disparity between the value placed on the life of a Briton and that of a Saxon";[209] while for Härke Ine's laws "confirm the lower status of the natives."[210]

The evidence of the laws themselves is less certain than those conclusions. Only nine (seven per cent) of the 119 clauses in the laws of Ine mention people called *wealh (or wilisc)* and those called *englisc*. The remaining 110 clauses do not specify any such distinction. Both terms are absent in the three Kentish law codes even though Kent is believed to have been one of the earliest regions to be settled by Germanic immigrants. This is a remarkably slight foundation for the argument that politics, society and economy in early medieval England was structured on the basis of ethnicity.

The nine clauses fall into three groups. The first related to wergilds, payments of compensation for crimes against a person. They list wergilds of -*wealh* with a holding of half a hide, one hide, or five hides and that of a *wealh gafolgelda* (clauses 24.2, 32, 23.3). The three distinctive characteristics of that first group signal ancient free landholdings whose origins were rooted in traditional Romano-British law: -*wealh* was a person, community, or institution whose legal position was rooted in late Romano-British customary traditions; hides were units of assessment of the value of characteristic public obligations that a free landholding—varying in area from very small to extensive—owed to a territory or a king. Some were rendered in kind, others in service, and yet others—like the *gafol*, a distinctive early public payment—were made in coin.[211] "Possession of a hide," says Faith, "was the qualification for free status and membership of the community," and the obligations attached to it (like the payment of *gafol*) were the outward signals of that status.[212] Both individually and together those three characteristics suggest that wergilds covered by those three clauses were being articulated in terms of the ancient connection in existing customary law between landholding, status, and public obligation. In all other clauses, wergilds were a reflection of an individual's social status, depending on whether he was (for instance) a *ceorl* or an *eorl*.

The second group has just one instance (clause 33): it recorded the wergild of a high-ranking royal official whose title was the king's *horswealh*. Its meaning remains obscure. Faull has suggested that he may have been a senior official at court, perhaps something like the master of the king's horse. The -*wealh* suffix implies that the origins of the role may have lain in late Romano-British tradition.[213] It persisted into the late ninth century when the death in 897 of Wulfric, King Alfred's *horsðegn*, was sufficiently important to be recorded in the *Anglo-Saxon Chronicle*.[214]

The third group consists of three clauses each making it easier to accuse *wiliscne* than *engliscne* slaves.[215] The first (clause 54.2) required a lower property guarantee against false accusation of a *wiliscne* than for an *engliscne* slave; the remaining two (clauses 74–74.2) outlined processes and compensations that followed from the murder of an *Englisce mon* by a *wealh* slave.

There are at least three ways in which those nine clauses might be interpreted:

- Perhaps *engliscne* were higher in status than *wiliscne*, and maybe their lives were therefore worth more. That system of value is reflected in modern tariffs for robbery, for instance, in which targeting high value goods is one of the criteria for the determination of a high level of harm.[216]

- Or, second, perhaps the clauses were intended to deter discrimination against *engliscne*. Laws can employ the carrot as well as the stick. For example, levels of British vehicle taxation link carbon-dioxide emissions in car exhausts with protection of the environment. They begin by offering inducements for good behaviour:

cars which produce between zero and fifty grammes of carbon dioxide per km are liable for the lowest tax. At the upper end of the scale, cars producing around five times as much carbon dioxide as those in the lowest group are liable for around two hundred times as much in tax.[217] By analogy, it is possible that Ine's laws were designed to protect *engliscne* from unfounded accusations to which, for whatever reason, they may have been more vulnerable;

- Or perhaps the clauses simply restate long-standing traditions of Romano-British customary law. It has already been noted that, where the *wergild* of *wealh* is explicitly stated, it is based on the size of an individual's *landholdings*. Where wergild is not qualified by ethnicity, it reflects an individual's *status*—for example, that of *ceorls* or *geneats*. Maybe traditional compensations attached to *-wealh* landholdings were set by ancient customary tradition, while the remainder (articulated in terms of social position) were adaptations to new conditions? That is, perhaps the laws illustrate the growing hierarchical complexity that marks the transition from late antique to early medieval England.

We simply do not know which, if any, of those interpretations is correct. There is nothing in the clauses in Ine's law code to support the assumption that they are evidence of a society structured in terms of distinctive ethnicities—unless one also believes that the code was drawn up solely by and for ethnically defined "Anglo-Saxons" and for that, too, there is no evidence. This is not to say that there is no evidence of ethnicity in those clauses; clearly there is. What is missing is evidence of a society socially and legally predicated upon it.

Gens, Nationes, and Populi

Scholars have also turned their attention to the Latin terms *gens, nationes,* and *populi* in the earliest versions of the works of Gildas and Bede. They were initially interpreted as making ethnic distinctions between early medieval groups who defined themselves in terms of their ancestry or place of origin. More recently, however, the scholarly consensus has come to see them as "signals of markers of legal obligation" that communities owed to different authorities at different scales under customary law. [218] *Gens*, *nationes*, or *populi* might, they suggest, more accurately be translated as "community" of one sort or another rather than as "the people of a nation."[219] They reveal something about how power was perceived at the time, but do not suggest that ethnicity was significant in those claims. That is, the use of such words may have been generalized, being elastic terms used to refer to a range of groups holding bundles of rights in different contexts and across geographic scales.[220] Bede's *gens Anglorum* was thus the community that adhered to the Roman (as opposed to the Celtic) church, rendered the obligations the church required, and structured religious observation according to its customary traditions.[221] Modern communities demonstrate the same variety, explaining their participation in terms of governance as local, parochial, district, county, regional, or (inter)national; in terms of belief (church, diocese, archbishopric, for instance); in terms of activity (local, regional, and (inter)national clubs and societies of all kinds); and so on.[222] It is difficult to go much further. Geary, for instance, has concluded that "we have no possibility of determining whether such an identity or identities did exist, who held them or what the contradictions, tensions, and dynamic processes within this putative identity may have been."[223]

Brittonic, Old English, and Spoken Latin

One of the standard arguments to support arguments for the division of early medieval communities on ethnic lines is based on the early dominance of Old English (see Chapter 2, above). Linguists generally explain the emergence of English as the reflection of what they assume was its higher social and legal status compared with Brittonic.[224] They suggest that OE originated as a Germanic language spoken by those of high status. It was bowdlerized by socially inferior adults whose first language was Brittonic and who learned it imperfectly as a second language through which they were compelled to communicate with their new masters. Their inevitable syntactical errors became fixed in their transmission of OE to their children and other descendants. Those, in turn, gradually moved to speaking it as a first language in an attempt "to gain access to the social benefits associated with prestige status" of the Anglo-Saxon elite.[225] That process is believed to explain the "moderately heavy substratum influence [of Brittonic] especially in the syntax [structure] and phonology [pronunciation]" of Old English.[226] Those conclusions are, it is argued, supported by the relative paucity of Brittonic loan words in Old English, a conclusion which is becoming less secure in light of the growing number of place-names in which Brittonic elements are being recognized.[227]

The model of colonial transmission is based on four assumptions: first, that there were social divisions structured around ethnicity in early medieval England; second, that Brittonic was the principal language of late Roman Britain; third, that OE was the earliest Germanic language to be spoken in Britain; and fourth, that language is an index of ethnicity. The first two assumptions have already been addressed and found wanting, and the third remains contested (see Chapter 2, 'Language', above). The fourth assumption, that "the Anglo-Saxons" only spoke Germanic and that their insistence on the language was one of the signals of their ethnicity, is also problematic. There is no innate link between language and ethnicity, especially in a bi- or multilingual society. There is, after all, considerable evidence that many communities across the period were bilingual and may, indeed, have spoken several languages. Brittonic and OE place-name elements occur, for instance, in an intermingled distribution across the East Anglian fen basin, across which Brittonic continued to be spoken at least into the eighth century and perhaps later.[228] Whether the emergence of OE can be taken as evidence of structured ethnicity is uncertain. Individuals able to speak two or more languages will generally use the language that is most effective in a particular context at a particular time.

Genetic Research

Some recent genetic research has attempted to measure the extent of fifth- and sixth-century "Anglo-Saxon" migration into Britain, and to model the period in which assimilation occurred between supposedly separate late Romano-British and immigrant populations. It assumes that early medieval migration was unusual in its scale and in the cultural cohesion of the immigrants, and that there was antagonistic division between Brittonic- and Old English-speaking communities (see "The Evidence of Genetic and Isotopic Research," above). That research concluded that intermarriage between British and north-west European immigrants occurred in the mid-ninth century.[229] The time-lag between the *adventus*, believed to have taken place in the fifth and sixth centuries, and assimilation three hundred or so years later thus required explanation. It came in the proposition that British communities and Germanic immigrants remained sufficiently formally separated over those three hundred years to prevent assimilation.

The structures of apartheid formally imposed in South Africa between 1948 and 1994 are occasionally used as an analogous example.[230] That suggestion can rapidly be dismissed. Apartheid was a system based on the plainly wrong and deeply pernicious belief that cultural characteristics could be identified with visible physical characteristics. That is not the same as the basis in the similarly flawed construct of ethnicity proposed for early medieval England. Apartheid depended on complex, highly structured, interconnected state institutions. They included: extensive, detailed, discriminatory legislation enacted to control all aspects of an individual's life—including legal rights, place of residence, personal relationships, employment, access to amenities, public behaviour and so on; support for that legislation from an extensive administrative and technical bureaucracy that included large numbers of informers; and its systematic enforcement through institutionalized state violence whose repertoire included (but was not restricted to) indefinite detention without trial, isolation and banishment, torture and murder. There is no evidence for any of these structures or mechanisms as a means for dividing communities in terms of their ethnicity in early medieval England.

The apartheid model is also empirically contradicted by the results of isotope analysis of dental enamel from early Anglo-Saxon burials (see pp. 40–41, above).[231] They show that most people in fifth- and sixth-century cemeteries were locally born and brought up; that those from outside Britain were buried among them, and could not be distinguished by any different sort of burial rite—that is, that they had been assimilated into local communities; and that, contrary to expectations, many of those immigrants originated not only in north-west Europe but also in north Africa, the southern Mediterranean, the near East, and other parts of Europe.[232] They cannot have spoken a common language, shared common traditions, held the same beliefs, or used the same kinds of objects in the same kinds of ways; and even those who did speak the same language and/or shared the same material culture may have regarded themselves as belonging to different groups.[233] The incongruity of the proposition of a common identity among early medieval migrants is clear from the analogy with, for instance, modern migrants into Britain in the last quarter of 2016: while forty-three percent came from across Europe, they arrived from Greece to Finland, and from Latvia to Spain; the remaining fifty-seven percent came from 114 countries and every continent.[234]

Despite the application of all the powers and levers of a complex twentieth-century state apartheid was visibly unsuccessful. How could it have worked in Anglo-Saxon England where any such institutions were lacking and where the state was insufficiently evolved to create or support them? As Reynolds has commented, "Apartheid is hard enough to maintain even when physical differences are obvious, political control is firm, and records of births, deaths, and marriages are kept."[235] Nor is there any evidence of the legislation and/or any other means for its enforcement. The term is, moreover, laden with further meanings which cannot apply here. Its use is as inappropriate, offensive, and tasteless as any analogy with discrimination against Jews in Nazi Germany might be. The analogy should permanently be discarded.

There is little evidence to support the proposition that ethnicity was a fundamental value around which late antique or early medieval society, political authority, or economic production was structured. This is not the same as saying that it did not exist or was not an aspect of identity at the time. Without more solid evidence is difficult, however, to accept it as a premise for historical interpretation.

The Model of "Elite Replacement"

Growing evidence of the numerical disparity between a large post-Roman population and relatively limited fifth- and sixth-century immigration into Britain, and for the cultural diversity of incomers, posed a problem for explanations demanding a leading role for Germanic ethnicity in the emergence of Anglo-Saxon identity. There could not have been enough Anglo-Saxons to drive out Romano-British communities; both groups must have lived alongside each other and, in this case, the supposed dominance of the former needed another explanation. The model of "elite replacement" offered a way to bridge that gap. It did so through two propositions: that the Romano-British leaders of late antique communities were rapidly, sometimes forcibly, replaced by "Anglo-Saxon" rulers; and that the latter used their "Anglo-Saxon" ethnicity to signal their special status in active resistance to any form of assimilation with a more adaptable late Romano-British society (see also "Ethnogenesis," below).[236] The dominance of Germanic material culture and of the Old English language could thus be explained in terms of their adoption by those of lower status and Romano-British origin who aspired towards the upward mobility, wealth, and patronage exhibited by their "Anglo-Saxon" leaders.[237]

There are a number of problems with that model. The first is, as outlined above, that there are no obvious observable differences between supposed "British" and "Germanic" communities or individuals in the archaeology of the fifth or sixth centuries or later: they lived in and farmed the same landscapes in the same ways, and were buried in the same places with the same kinds of goods. There are, of course, differences from one part of England to another in typologies of artifact and in customary behaviour of various kinds—like burial or the morphology of field systems. But while it is possible that these may be evidence of ethnicity, they may simply be evidence of regional distributions of particular sets of artifact, or individual expressions of wealth or status. If elites were so parochially, so indefatigably, Germanic in outlook that the only way in which lesser men could retain influence, possibly even their livelihoods, was by adopting the language, customs, and material culture of their leaders this is not visible in the archaeological evidence either generally or in a distinction that can convincingly be claimed as ethnic between the burials of some, wealthier, individuals compared with the generality of those in early cemeteries.[238]

A second problem is that across England kings from the fifth century until the eighth and beyond continued to position themselves as the heirs of Rome.[239] In the two centuries after 400 many had Latin names: Ambrosius Aurelianus in the fifth century, Aircol (Agricola) Llauhir around 500, and Gildas' own contemporary, Constantine of Dumnonia.[240] The epigraphic evidence, too, is largely written in Latin and uses Latin forms.[241] The assemblage and character of the royal regalia excavated at Sutton Hoo referenced Roman antecedents, their owners perhaps using them to "dress up as Romans—claiming a right to rule as the spiritual descendants of the Roman emperors."[242] The earliest Christian kings of Kent, Northumbria, and Deira were buried in the *porticus* of their principal minsters, emulating royal mausolea in Rome, and built churches whose design was based on Roman *basilica* used for civilian assembly, while the monumental architecture of early medieval palaces, too, may have been based on the forms and layouts of Roman villas.[243] All appear to be deliberate references to *Romanitas*.[244] They offer qualified support to the suggestion that as late as the seventh and eighth centuries England "can still be regarded as culturally late Roman" given that there appears to have been some sense of the continued importance, in some contexts, of conforming at least in part to an idea of "being Roman" (although that should be qualified by saying that it was almost certainly based on contemporary beliefs of what "being Roman" meant rather than what it necessarily was either at the time or had been in the past).[245] This is a long way from the unsullied Germanic status that such elites were supposed to have insisted upon.

A third problem lies in that most intimate signal of individuals' identities: their personal names. Cerdic (d. 554) and his successor Cynric (d. 581), the two sixth-century kings who were supposed to have founded the "Anglo-Saxon" kingdom of Wessex, confusingly both had Brittonic names.[246] Other royal names combined an Old English element with -*wealh*, which signalled late Romano-British tradition. Well-known examples include *Cenwealh* (king of Wessex, d. 672), *Æðelwealh* (king of the south Saxons, d. ca. 685), *Merewalh* (d. late seventh century) who was a sub-king of the *Magonsæte*, and *Penwealh* (an early/mid seventh-century Mercian prince).[247] As late as 897 Wulfric—the leader of king Alfred's elite troop of horse—was, despite his Old English name, a Brittonic-speaking Welsh sub-king.[248] That is, the languages that contributed to the names of high status men from supposedly solidly "Anglo-Saxon" royal families do not appear to have been markers of their ethnicity. We have no real idea of how important ethnicity was in naming individuals.

Last is the problem of how such transitions in political control were implemented in practice. The administration of Roman Britain was based on a set of nested hierarchies: broadly speaking from *vicus*, a small local centre, to *pagus*, the locality, to *civitas*, a region often reproducing a prehistoric territory, to one of the two sub-provinces into which Roman Britain was divided from the early third century, and then to the province of Britain itself. Two sets of evidence for continuity in political structure suggest a degree of stability in many places across all levels of local administration for long enough for the names of such centres to be preserved in documentary evidence and/or in place-names. Kingdoms apparently led by late Romano-British kings have been documented across Britain in the fifth and sixth centuries—best known are those like Dyfed, Powys, and Gwynedd in Wales, Dumnonia in the south-west, or Rheged in the northwest; others in the east lay in the supposed heartlands of Anglo-Saxon settlement—in the kingdoms of Elmet, Lindsey, and even of East Anglia itself.[249] The Romano-British origins of lower-ranking regional polities is indicated in the -sæte suffix of such groups as the *Summersæte* in Somerset, *Magonsæte* in Herefordshire, *Chilternsæte* across the southern borders of Oxfordshire and Buckinghamshire, or the *Grantasæte* who controlled the Cam valley.[250] At the most local level, Margaret Gelling has argued that a number of *vici* survived for long enough across the whole of southern England, including the east, for their names to become incorporated in modern place names.[251] Taken as a whole, such evidence suggests a degree of stability across the administrative hierarchy from late Roman into early medieval England, variably manifested from one region to another. Roman and Byzantine influences contributed alongside those from north-west Europe to the evolution of late antique and early medieval English society, observable in everyday jewellery, weaponry, ceramics, and textiles, in specialist assemblages like military insignia, and in elite regalia, architecture, and designed landscapes. If ethnicity was really the basis of post-Roman leadership and political identity, it has yet to be convincingly demonstrated.

Ethnogenesis: The Deliberate Construction of a Pragmatically Hybrid Political Identity

The interval between the supposed beginning of the *adventus* together with concerns about the literal interpretation of the early sources, led to the revival of an older explanatory model: that is, as the early kingdoms emerged towards the end of the sixth century, their new kings sought to consolidate their authority by encouraging the deliberate creation of myths of the origins and history of their royal dynasties that amounted to "a consciously-structured narrative sufficient to bind entire communities, and vehicles to perpetuate those myths," a process known as ethnogensis.[252] That approach is once more founded on the premise of ethnicity. Its underlying proposition is that elite warrior bands from north-west Europe, who settled in and then occupied fifth- and sixth-century England under their own leaders, were bearers (*Traditionsträger*) of the core traditional beliefs that made up their "Germanic" identity.[253] Each group deliberately built on those traditions to develop a cohesive cultural identity constructed of interconnected religious, mythic, genealogical, historical, and ethnic narratives that rationalized and supported their political authority, and that ethnicity was then extended to include those over whom they reigned.[254] Halsall, for instance, has argued that it was freemen rather than the generality of the population who "played an important role in maintaining the exclusivity of their ethnic identity."[255]

The conceptual problem with the model of ethnogenesis is that, although it appears to offer an innovative social and cultural argument for understanding the emergence of the English, that appearance is flawed. Its deliberate focus on Germanic tradition retains ethnicity at its core.[256] That inevitably leads to a circularity of its arguments: early records are interpreted as evidence of ethnicity; the evidence is mined in the anticipation of finding corroboration; and, when it is found, is interpreted as fulfilling that expectation.[257]

The documentary evidence for the extension of core Germanic traditions into late antique and early medieval identity is, furthermore, problematic. While it is true that early origin myths and genealogies are at first sight flagrantly Germanic, many are as startlingly British in origin as the names of their kings discussed above—that is, their content belies their stated purpose. Oral histories later incorporated into the *Anglo-Saxon Chronicle*, for example, told how Cerdic and his son Cynric arrived on a Hampshire beach with three shiploads of warriors in 495/6, going on over the next six years to conquer the region that they formed into the kingdom of Wessex. Yet, confusingly, the names of these north-west European leaders were not Germanic, but Brittonic. This suggests that, by the time that the narrative history of the early kings of Wessex was formalized—perhaps at the late seventh-century court of King Ine—neither the bard nor his audience thought that ethnicity was signaled by the languages from which personal names were drawn.[258] The mythical ancestors of the early kings of Wessex, their carefully constructed regnal dates, and the lengths of their reigns were polished again at the late ninth-century court of King Alfred to provide support for his own political ambitions.[259] The regnal lists for Lindsey, Mercia, and Bernicia received similarly creative treatment.[260] And the origins of the kings of Kent recorded by Bede in 731 suggest that their origins, too, lay in a "fiction of epic heroes, gods and demi-gods" and equally fictitious heroic leaders that were common currency at early eighth century royal courts.[261] The strength of the documentary evidence for ethnogenesis is doubtful.

There is, finally, a mismatch between supposedly core Germanic cultural traditions and attempts by early medieval English kings symbolically to underscore the legitimacy of their authority by re-utilizing or constructing archaeological landscapes.[262] Prehistoric and Romano-British barrows, standing stones, and other ancient monuments were re-used in demarcating early medieval territorial boundaries.[263] The secondary placement of many late antique and early medieval burials in prehistoric barrows on the skylines of southern Sussex may, Semple has suggested, have been a means of asserting a visible statement of their lordship across the cultural viewsheds of many communities.[264] Other well-known examples include secondary burials inserted into prehistoric and Roman barrows on the Yorkshire Wolds and the elite burial set into an earlier barrow at Swallowcliffe Down (Wiltshire).[265] Royal barrows at Sutton Hoo (Suffolk) and Taplow (Buckinghamshire), for instance, may have been constructed specifically to give them the appearance of antiquity.[266] Bradley has pointed out that the location, layout, and zoned usage of the seventh- and eighth-century royal complex at Yeavering was determined by the presence of two nearby prehistoric monuments, a Bronze Age stone circle and a barrow of the same period, both of which were re-used as post-Roman cemeteries.[267] Indeed, Geary has argued that such selective adaptations of older elements in the landscape "was really equivalent to the composition of prestigious but fictitious genealogies" in which a late British past was more significant than any supposed Germanic antecedents.[268]

Discussion

There is little archaeological, documentary, linguistic, or genomic evidence to support the proposition that ethnicity was a fundamental value around which early medieval society, political authority, or economic production was structured. It cannot be used as a premise in interpreting the period without firm evidence.

The alternative possibility that existing cultural and political traditions could be adapted to changing circumstance provides a rich new seam for research.[269] That conclusion is illustrated in the unselfconscious amalgamation of cultural references of the Repton Stone, a fragment of an early eighth-century cross that once stood outside the royal Mercian mausoleum at Repton (Figure 4). The figure is believed to represent Æthelbald, king of Mercia, who died in 757, and offers a rare opportunity to see the "Anglo-Saxon" elite as they wished to be perceived in life since it preserves details of hair, grooming, and posture that are lost after death. The movement of the horse, its saddle, and the rider's stance upon it, his full-face portrait, pleated skirt, neat hair, and diadem are all drawn from late Roman imperial models, by that period focused on Byzantium; the moustache is an inheritance from both British and Germanic traditions; the figure's hose and shirt may be Germanic in style, like the *seax* carried at his waist.[270] The figure's confident statement of identity does not proselytize a Germanic ethnicity. Instead, it includes a range of cultural references—some from late Roman Britain, others from the empire, and yet others reflecting the growing prominence of contacts across the North Sea region.

Figure 4. The "Repton Stone" is a fragment of an early eighth-century cross from the royal Mercian mausoleum at Repton. Believed to represent Æthelbald, king of Mercia from 716 to 757, it combines insular, Byzantine and north-west European cultural references (photograph © Dr Heidi Stoner 2017, reproduced with permission).

Such conclusions suggest the possibility that social identity could be both fluid and dynamic adjusted by place and time rather than necessarily fixed in conceptions on ethnicity. Geary, for instance, has concluded that "Membership in a barbarian people depended more on willingness to identify with the traditions of that people—incarnated in its political leadership, that is, royal or aristocratic families, and its ability to contribute to that tradition, essentially through military service—than on biological descent, culture, language, or geographical origin."[271] The identification of the names of fifth- and sixth-century folk groups offers that position some support. Their names suggest that they identified themselves in terms of the local landscapes that provided their livelihoods rather than in terms of ethnicity: the *Gyrwe* who occupied the fen-edge north and south of the river Nene were those with rights to exploit the wetland pastures that lay to the east of Peterborough; the *Hæslingas* (Haslingfield, Cambridgeshire) defined themselves in terms of the extensive *feld*, large areas of common grazing that lay along the valley floor of one of the tributaries of the river Cam.[272]

This is not to argue that the political transition of the fifth century was without turmoil, that there was no change, or that ethnicity was or was not an influence. It does suggest that the concept is sufficiently problematic to be unsuitable as an explanatory paradigm for the emergence of the English. As Reynolds has succinctly pointed out, "We might do well to remember that the early medieval English did not call themselves Anglo-Saxons. If we want to call them that, we ought to think hard about what we mean, and what others may think we mean, by the name that we have chosen to use."[273]

Notes

[175] There is an enormous literature on early medieval identity and ethnicity. For critical evaluations of the concept in this context see, for example, Susan Reynolds, "What Do We Mean by 'Anglo-Saxon' and 'Anglo-Saxons'?," *Journal of British Studies* 24, 4 (1985): 395–414; Stephen Harris, *Race and Ethnicity in Anglo-Saxon Literature* (New York: Routledge, 2003), chap. 1; William Frazier and Andrew Tyrell, ed., *Social Identity in Early Medieval Britain* (Leicester: Leicester University Press, 2000); Andrew Gillett, "Was Ethnicity Politicized in the Earliest Medieval Kingdoms?," in *On Barbarian Identity. Critical Approaches to Ethnicity in the Early Middle Ages*, ed. Andrew Gillett (Turnhout: Brepols, 2002), 85–122, at 85–86; Stefan Brather, "Ethnic Identities as Constructions of Archaeology: The case of the Alamanni," in *On Barbarian Identity. Critical Approaches to Ethnicity in the Early Middle Ages*, ed. Andrew Gillett (Turnhout: Brepols, 2002), 149–76; Halsall, *Barbarian Migrations*, 16–38; James, *Europe's Barbarians*, 105–23; Walter Pohl, "Comparing Communities—the Limits of Typology," *History and Anthropology* 26, 1 (2015): 18–35; Susanne Hakenbeck, "Roman or Barbarian? Shifting Identities in Early Medieval Cemeteries in Bavaria," *Post-Classical Archaeologies* 1 (2011): 37–66; Patrick Geary, "Power and Ethnicity, History and Anthropology," *History and Anthropology* 26, 1 (2015): 8–17.

[176] F. Barth, ed., *Ethnic Groups and Boundaries: The Social Organisation of Cultural Difference* (Boston: Little, Brown, 1969).

[177] For example, Catherine Hills, "Overview: Anglo-Saxon Identity," in *The Oxford Handbook of Anglo-Saxon Archaeology*, ed. David Hinton, Helena Hamerow, and Sally Crawford (Oxford: Oxford University Press, 2011), 3–12; Walter Goffart, "The Barbarians in Late Antiquity and How They Were Accommodated in the West," in *Debating the Middle Ages: Issues and Readings*, ed. Lester Little and Barbara Rosenwein (Oxford: Oxford University Press, 1998), 25–44; Pohl, "Ethnic Names and Identities."

[178] For example, Halsall, *Barbarian Migrations*, 60–62.

[179] Hakenbeck, "Roman or Barbarian," at 39.

[180] Harrington and Welch, *Early Anglo-Saxon Kingdoms*, 6.

[181] Charles-Edwards, *Wales and the Britons*, 48; Barbara Yorke, *Kings and Kingdoms of Early Anglo-Saxon England* (London: Routledge, 1990), 5–7; James, *Europe's Barbarians*, 202–4; Gerrard, *Ruin of Roman Britain*, 252–62.

[182] Barbara Yorke, *Wessex in the Early Middle Ages* (Leicester: Leicester University Press, 1995), 32.

[183] Harrington and Welch, *Early Anglo-Saxon Kingdoms*, 6.

[184] Green, *Britons and Anglo-Saxons,* 87.

[185] Roger White, "Managing Transition: Western Britain from the End of the Roman Empire to the Rise of Penda," *History Compass* 11, 8 (2013): 584–96.

[186] Sarah Semple, *Perceptions of the Prehistoric in Anglo-Saxon England: Religion, Ritual, and Rulership in the Landscape* (Oxford: Oxford University Press, 2013), 27. See also Bruce Eagles, "Lindsey," in *The Origins of the Anglo-Saxon Kingdoms*, ed. Steven Bassett (Leicester: Leicester University Press, 1989), 202–12; David Dumville, "The Origins of Northumbria: Some Aspects of the British Background," in *The Origins of the Anglo-Saxon Kingdoms*, ed. Steven Bassett (Leicester: Leicester University Press, 1989), 213–24. For a critique of these views see, for example, John Moreland, "Ethnicity, Power and the English," in *Social Identity in Early Medieval Britain*, ed. William Frazier and Andrew Tyrell (Leicester: Leicester University Press, 2000), 23–52.

[187] John Hines, "The Origins of East Anglia in a North Sea Zone," in *East Anglia and its North Sea World in the Middle Ages*, ed. David Bates and Robert Liddiard (Woodbridge: Boydell and Brewer, 2013), 16–43, at 39. The initial proposition was that of Leeds, "The Distribution of the Angles and Saxons." See also, for example, Thomas Charles-Edwards, *After Rome* (Oxford: Oxford University Press, 2003), 88–89; Gerrard, *Ruin of Roman Britain*, 202–3. Toby Martin, *The Cruciform Brooch and Anglo-Saxon England* (Woodbridge: Boydell and Brewer, 2015) offers a further convincing challenge to the orthodoxy.

[188] Hines, "Origins of East Anglia," at 21.

[189] Hines, "Origins of East Anglia," at 28–30.

[190] Martin Henig, *The Art of Roman Britain* (London: Routledge, 1995), 170–72.

[191] Henig, *Art of Roman Britain*, 170, see also 171–72.

[192] "Bede, The Lives of the Holy Abbots of Weremouth and Jarrow," in *Ecclesiastical History of the English Nation*, trans. J. A. Giles (London: Dent, 1910), 349–66, at chaps. 5 and 6 (for masons and glaziers see chap. 5, for the chanter see chap. 6).

[193] The underlying map is based on Williamson, "East Anglia's character and the 'North Sea World'," at 45. North lies at the bottom of the map which is, in conventional terms, upside-down in order so that the North Sea and the rivers leading to it become the map's focus rather than the landmasses that surround the North Sea.

[194] "World Cup 2018: How London's Swedish community is preparing for the Three Lions quarter-final," *London Evening Standard*, July 6, 2018, https://www.standard.co.uk/lifestyle/london-life/sweden-vs-england-world-cup-swedish-in-london-a3881151.html.

[195] Moreland, "Ethnicity, Power and the English," 29–31. David Austin, "The 'Proper Study' of Medieval Archaeology," in *From the Baltic to the Black Sea. Studies in Medieval Archaeology*, ed. David Austin and Leslie Alcock (London: Unwin, 1990), 9–42, at 14–19.

[196] Goffart, *Barbarian Tides*, 4; see also Gillett, "Ethnogenesis," at 250–52.

[197] Angela Reyes, "Language and Ethnicity," in *Sociolinguistics and Language Education*, ed. Nancy Hornberger and Sandra McKay (Bristol: Multilingual Matters, 2010), 398–426, at 401; see also Paul Gilroy, *There Ain't No Black in the Union Jack: The Cultural Politics of Race and Nation* (London: Hutchinson, 1987), 66.

[198] See, for example, Reynolds, *Kingdoms and Communities*, 225; Michael Kulikowski, "Nation versus Army: A Necessary Contrast?," in *On Barbarian Identity. Critical Approaches to Ethnicity in the Middle Ages*, ed. Andrew Gillett (Turnhout: Brepols, 2002), 69–84.

[199] Susan Reynolds, *Kingdoms and Communities in Western Europe, 900–1300* (Oxford: Clarendon Press, 1984), 225.

[200] See Christopher Scull, "Archaeology, Early Anglo-Saxon Society and the Origins of Anglo-Saxon Kingdoms," *Anglo-Saxon Studies in Archaeology and History* 6 (1993): 66–82; Harrington and Welch, *Early Anglo-Saxon Kingdoms*; Yorke, *Wessex in the Early Middle Ages*, 50–51.

[201] See, for example, Maitland, *Domesday Book*, 222; Higham, *Rome, Britain*, 226, 234 and chap. 8; Bryan Ward-Perkins, "Why Did the Anglo-Saxons Not Become More British?," *English Historical Review* 115, 462 (2000): 513–33; Tristram, "Why Don't the English Speak Welsh?"

[202] David Wilson, ed. *The Archaeology of Anglo-Saxon England* (London: Methuen, 1976), 4. See also Martin Carver, "Kingship and Material Culture," in *The Origins of the Anglo-Saxon Kingdoms*, ed. Steven Bassett (Leicester: Leicester University Press, 1989), 141–58, at 156; Higham, *Rome, Britain*, 233.

[203] Ward-Perkins, "Why Did the Anglo-Saxons Not Become More British?," at 514. See also Higham, *Rome, Britain*, 226.

[204] See, for example, Yorke, *Kings and Kingdoms*, 5; Carver, "Kingship and Material Culture," at 156; Higham, *Rome, Britain*, 226 and 233; Pohl, "Comparing Communities," at 31; Mark Thomas, Heinrich Härke, Gary German, and Michael Stumpf, "Limited Inter-

ethnic Marriage, Differential Reproductive Success and the Spread of 'Continental' Y Chromosomes in Early Anglo-Saxon England," in *Simulation, Genetics and Human Prehistory*, ed. S. Matsumura, Peter Forster, and Colin Renfrew (Cambridge: McDonald Institute for Archaeological Research, 2008), 61–70, at 66–67; John Davies, *A History of Wales* (London: Penguin, 1993, 2007 ed.); Alex Woolf, "Apartheid and Economics," in *Britons in Anglo-Saxon England*, ed. Nicholas Higham (Woodbridge: Boydell and Brewer, 2007), 115–29, at 129. There is an extended critique of this approach in Gerrard, *Ruin of Roman Britain*, 259–62.

[205] W. H. Auden, "An Improbable Life," *Forewords and Afterwords* (New York: Vintage, 1974), 302.

[206] "The Laws of Ine (688–694)." The other three law codes were those of Kentish kings: Æthelberht, in around 600; Hlothere and Eadric, in about 673 and 685; and Wihtred, in 695. See "From the Laws of Ethelbert, King of Kent (602–603?)," in *English Historical Documents c.500–1042*, 390–93; "The Laws of Hlothhere and Eadric, Kings of Kent (673–685?)," in *English Historical Documents*, ed. Dorothy Whitelock (London: Routledge, 1979), 393–95; "The Laws of Wihtred, King of Kent (695)," in *English Historical Documents c.500–1042*, ed. Dorothy Whitelock (London: Routledge, 1979), 396–99.

[207] Tom Lambert, *Law and Order in Anglo-Saxon England* (Oxford: Oxford University Press, 2017), 71–72, 99; see also his chaps. 1 and 2.

[208] Ward-Perkins, "Why Did the Anglo-Saxons Not Become More British?," at 524.

[209] Martin Grimmer, "Britons in Early Wessex: The Evidence of the Law Code of Ine," in *Britons in Anglo-Saxon England*, ed. Nicholas Higham (Woodbridge: Boydell and Brewer, 2007), 102–14, at 105.

[210] Heinrich Härke, "Anglo-Saxon Immigration and Ethnogenesis," *Medieval Archaeology* 55 (2011): 1–29, at 14.

[211] Charles-Edwards, *Wales and the Britons*, 1; Lambert, *Law and Order*, 92; Rosamond Faith, *The English Peasantry and the Growth of Lordship* (Leicester: Leicester University Press, 1997), 5, 106. See also Thomas Charles-Edwards, "Kinship, Status and the Origins of the Hide," *Past and Present* 56 (1972): 3–33.

[212] Faith, *English Peasantry*, 128.

[213] Margaret Faull, "The Semantic Development of Old English *wealh*," *Leeds Studies in English*, n.s. 8 (1975): 20–44, at 28–29.

[214] *Anglo-Saxon Chronicles*, ed. Michael Swanton (London: Phoenix, 2000), 91.

[215] "The Laws of Ine (688–694)"; *Die Gesetze der Angelsachsen*, 88–123.

[216] For example, Sentencing Council, *Robbery. Definitive Guidance* (London: Sentencing Council, 2016), 11. https://www.sentencingcouncil.org.uk/wp-content/uploads/Robbery-offences-definitive-guideline-web.pdf.

[217] UK Government, *Vehicle Tax Rate Tables*, https://www.gov.uk/vehicle-tax-rate-tables.

[218] Reynolds, "'Anglo-Saxon' and 'Anglo-Saxons'?," at 401. For interpretations of these terms as expressions of ethnicity see, for example, Pohl, "Comparing Communities," at 27; W. Trent Foley and Nicholas Higham, "Bede on the Britons," *Early Medieval Europe* 17, 2 (2009): 154–85. For interpretations in terms of community see, for example, Faith, *English Peasantry*, 2; Geary, *Myth of Nations*, 62; Moreland, "Ethnicity, Power and the English," at 46; Brather, "Ethnic Identities," at 149–50; Harris, *Race and Ethnicity*, 750; Stephen Harris, "An Overview of Race and Ethnicity in Pre-Norman England," *Literature Compass* 5 (2008): 1–15, at 11; James, *Europe's Barbarians*, 111; Hall, "Interlinguistic Communication"; Geary, "Power and Ethnicity."

[219] Reynolds, "'Anglo-Saxon' and 'Anglo-Saxons'," at 401. See also Andrew Gillett, "Ethnogenesis: A Contested Model of Early Medieval Europe," *History Compass* 4, 2 (2006): 241–60.

[220] Susan Reynolds, "Our Forefathers? Tribes, Peoples, Nations in the Historiography of the Age of Migrations," in Susan Reynolds, *The Middle Ages without Feudalism*, chap. 11 (Farnham: Ashgate Variorum, 2005), 22; Brather, "Ethnic Identities," at 150; Wormald, "Bede, the *Bretwaldas*," at 118; Geary, *Myth of Nations*, 62; Harris, *Race and Ethnicity*, 41.

[221] For example, Harris, "An Overview of Race and Ethnicity," at 10; Hall, "Interlinguistic Communication"; Wormald, "Bede, the *Bretwaldas*."

[222] Susan Reynolds, "Our Forefathers? Tribes, Peoples, Nations," at 22–25.

[223] Geary, "Power and Ethnicity," at 15.

[224] For example, Ward-Perkins, "Why Did the Anglo-Saxons Not Become More British?"; Coates, "Invisible Britons."

[225] Tristram, "Why Don't the English Speak Welsh?," at 202. See also Woolf, "Apartheid and Economics"; Charles-Edwards, *Wales and the Britons*, 88.

[226] Juhani Klemola, "English as a Contact Language in the British Isles," in *English as a Contact Language*, ed. Daniel Schreier and Marianne Hundt (Cambridge: Cambridge University Press, 2015), 75–87, at 75, my additions. See also Markku Filppula, Juhani Flemola, and Heli Paulasto, ed., *English and Celtic in Contact* (London: Routledge, 2007).

[227] Charles-Edwards, *Wales and the Britons*, 88; Coates, "Invisible Britons"; Richard Coates and Andrew Breeze, *Celtic Voices, English Places: Studies of the Celtic Impact on Place-Names in Britain* (Stamford: Shaun Tyas, 2000); Hall, "Interlinguistic Communication," 37–80; Gilroy, *There Ain't No Black*, 4.

[228] Charles-Edwards, *Wales and the Britons*, 75; Oosthuizen, *Anglo-Saxon Fenland*, chap. 3. There were Brittonic speakers in Hertfordshire until at least the seventh century: Kevin Fitzpatrick-Matthews, "The Experience of 'Small Towns': Utter Devastation, Slow Fading or Business as Usual?," in *AD 410: The History and Archaeology of Late Roman and Post-Roman Britain*, ed. Fiona Haarer and Rob Collins (London: Society for the Promotion of Roman Studies, 2014), 43–60, at 52.

[229] Weale, et al., "Y-chromosome Evidence"; Capelli, et al., "Y-chromosome Census"; Leslie, et al., "The Fine-Scale Genetic Structure." For a critical evaluation of this research, see Chapter 2, above, 'Evidence of Genetic and Isotopic Research' .

[230] Higham, *Rome, Britain*, 193; Mark Thomas, M. Stumpf, and Heinrich Härke, "Evidence for an Apartheid-like Social Structure in Early Anglo-Saxon England," *Proceedings of the Royal Society* B 273 (2006): 2651–57; Woolf, "Apartheid and Economics"; Härke, "Anglo-Saxon Immigration," at 1. For a contrary view see John Pattison, "Is it Necessary to Assume an Apartheid-like Social Structure in Early Anglo-Saxon England?," *Proceedings of the Royal Society* B 275 (2008): 2423–29, at 2425.

[231] Tooth enamel stores distinctive regional chemical markers created by variations in isotopes in water drunk during childhood.

[232] For further references see notes 150–52 above. See also Hemer, Evans, Chenery, et al., "Evidence of Early Medieval Trade"; Eckhardt, Müldner, and Lewis, "People on the Move"; Hughes, Millard, Lucy, et al., "Anglo-Saxon Origins."

[233] For example, Harris, *Race and Ethnicity*, 8; Geary, *Myth of Nations*, 37–38; Goffart, *Barbarian Tides*.

[234] UK Office for National Statistics, "Migration Statistics Quarterly Report: May 2017," https://www.ons.gov.uk/peoplepopulationandcommunity/populationandmigration/internationalmigration/bulletins/migrationstatisticsquarterlyreport/may2017.

[235] Reynolds, "'Anglo-Saxon' and 'Anglo-Saxons'?," at 402–3.

[236] Tristram, "Why Don't the English Speak Welsh?," at 214; see also Loveluck and Laing, "Britons and Saxons," at 538. See also Higham, *Rome, Britain*, chap. 8; John Hines, "The Beginning of the English: Identity, Material Culture and Language in Anglo-

Saxon England," *Anglo-Saxon Studies in Archaeology and History* 7 (1994): 49–59; Christopher Scull, "Approaches to Material Culture and Social Dynamics of the Migration Period of Eastern England," in *Europe Between Late Antiquity and the Middle Ages*, ed. John Bintliff and Helena Hamerow, BAR International Series, S617 (Oxford: British Archaeological Reports, 1995), 71–83.

[237] For example, Paul Barnwell, "Introduction," in *Political Assemblies in the Earlier Middle Ages*, ed. Paul Barnwell and Marco Mostert (Turnhout: Brepols, 2003), 1–10; Higham, *Rome, Britain*, chap. 8; Tristram, "Why Don't the English Speak Welsh?"; Woolf, "Apartheid and Economics."

[238] Lucy and Reynolds, "Burial in Early Medieval England," at 10; see Hughes, Millard, Lucy, et al., "Anglo-Saxon Origins."

[239] Gerrard, *Ruin of Roman Britain*, 195; Barbara Yorke, "The Burial of Kings in Anglo-Saxon England," in *Kingship, Legislation and Power in Anglo-Saxon England*, ed. Gale Owen-Crocker and Brian Schneider (Woodbridge: Boydell and Brewer 2013), 237–58, at 243; Tim Eaton, "Old Ruins New World," *British Archaeology* 60 (2001): 14–19.

[240] Gildas, *Ruin of Britain*, 25:3, 28–32.

[241] Charles-Edwards, *Wales and the Britons*, 116–73.

[242] J. Newman, "Sutton Hoo before Rædwald," *Current Archaeology* 180 (2002): 498–505, at 505.

[243] Yorke, "Burial of Kings," at 243, 247, 253; Michael Shapland, "The Cuckoo and the Magpie: The Building Culture in the Anglo-Saxon Church," in *The Material Culture of the Built Environment in the Anglo-Saxon World*, ed. Maren Clegg Hyer and Gale Owen-Crocker (Liverpool: Liverpool University Press, 2015), 92–116, at 106–9; Gerrard, *Ruin of Roman Britain*, 195.

[244] Martin Henig, "Remaining Roman in Britain AD 300–700: The Evidence of the Portable Art," in *Debating Late Antiquity in Britain AD 300–700*, ed. Rob Collins and James Gerrard, BAR British Series, 365 (Oxford: British Archaeological Reports, 2004), 13–24. See also Owen-Crocker, "British Wives and Slaves?"; Brather, "Acculturation and Ethnogenesis."

[245] Martin Henig, "Roman Britain after 410," *British Archaeology*, 68 (2002): 8–11, at 11. See also Walter Pohl, "Romanness: A Multiple Identity and its Changes," *Early Medieval Europe* 22, 4 (2014): 406–18.

[246] Dumville, "West Saxon Genealogical Regnal List," at 50–51.

[247] Kenneth Cameron, "The Meaning and Significance of Old English *Walh* in English Place-names," *Journal of the English Place-Name Society* 12 (1978–79): 1–46, at 5; Faull, "Old English *Wealh*,"

at 35; H. L. Gray, *English Field Systems* (London: Merlin, 1915); *Prosopography of Anglo-Saxon England,* www.pase.ac.uk.

[248] Faull, "Old English *Wealh*," at 28–30.

[249] Green, *Britons and Anglo-Saxons*; Damian Tyler, "Early Mercia and the Britons," in *Britons in Anglo-Saxon England,* ed. Nicholas Higham (Woodbridge: Boydell and Brewer, 2007), 91–101; Nellie Neilson, *A Terrier of Fleet, Lincolnshire* (London: British Academy, 1920); Nellie Neilson, *The Cartulary and Terrier of the Priory of Bilsington Kent* (London: British Academy, 1928); Reynolds, *Kingdoms and Communities*, 111, 138–39; Alan Everitt, *Continuity and Colonization: The Evolution of Kentish Settlement* (Leicester: Leicester University Press, 1986); David Roffe, "The Historical Context," in *Anglo-Saxon Settlement in the Siltland of Eastern England*, ed. Andy Crowson, Tom Lane, Ken Penn, and D. Trimble (Heckington: Lincolnshire Society for Archaeology and History, 2005), 264–88; Oosthuizen, *Anglo-Saxon Fenland*, chap. 4; Ian Roberts, "Re-thinking the Archaeology of Elmet," in *AD 410: The History and Archaeology of Late Roman and Post-Roman Britain*, ed. Fiona Haarer and Rob Collins (London: Society for the Promotion of Roman Studies, 2014), 182–94.

[250] C. R. Hart, "The Tribal Hidage," *Transactions of the Royal Historical Society*, Fifth Series, 21 (1971), 133–57; W. G. Hoskins and Douglas Stamp, *The Common Lands of England and Wales* (London: Department of the Environment, 1963), 7, 24; Susan Oosthuizen, "Prehistoric Fields into Medieval Furlongs? Evidence from Caxton, South Cambridgeshire," *Proceedings of the Cambridge Antiquarian Society*, 86 (1998): 145–52; Tyler, "Early Mercia and the Britons."

[251] Margaret Gelling, "English Place-names Derived from the Compound *Wīcham*," *Medieval Archaeology* 11 (1967): 87–104.

[252] See Gillett, "Ethnogenesis," at 244–45, and for a critical overview of the historiography. See also Geary, *Myth of Nations*; Goffart, *Barbarian Tides*; Dumville, "West Saxon Genealogical Regnal List."

[253] Gillett, "Ethnogenesis," at 246; James, *Europe's Barbarians*, 106–11.

[254] Charles Bowlus, "Ethnogenesis: The Tyranny of a Concept," in *On Barbarian Identity. Critical Approaches to Ethnicity in the Middle Ages*, ed. Andrew Gillett (Turnhout: Brepols, 2002), 241–56, at 245–46.

[255] Halsall, *Barbarian Migrations*, 18. See also Peter Heather, *The Goths* (Oxford: Blackwell, 1996), 301; Moreland, "Ethnicity, Power and the English," at 46.

[256] Gillett, "Ethnogenesis," at 253.

[257] This argument is explored at greater length in Gillett, "Ethnogenesis," at 50, 249.

[258] Dumville, "West Saxon Genealogical Regnal List."

[259] Dumville, "West Saxon Genealogical Regnal List," at 57.

[260] Dumville, "Kingship, Genealogies," at 80–81.

[261] Nicholas Brooks, "The Creation and Early Structure of the Kingdom of Kent," in *The Origins of the Anglo-Saxon Kingdoms*, ed. Steven Bassett (Leicester: Leicester University Press, 1989), 55–74, at 59.

[262] Semple, *Perceptions of the Prehistoric*, 6, 15–16; Howard Williams, "Monuments and the Past in Early Anglo-Saxon England," *World Archaeology* 30 (1998): 90–108, at 103; Richard Bradley, "Time Regained: The Creation of Continuity," *Journal of the British Archaeological Association* 140, 1 (1987): 1–17.

[263] Semple, *Perceptions of the Prehistoric*, 41–43.

[264] Semple, *Perceptions of the Prehistoric*, 24–25.

[265] Yorke, "Burial of Kings," at 240–43; Semple, *Perceptions of the Prehistoric*, 27–29.

[266] Yorke, "Burial of Kings," at 240–43; Semple, *Perceptions of the Prehistoric*, 27–29.

[267] Bradley, "Time Regained," at 5, 9; Yorke, "Burial of Kings," at 243.

[268] Geary, *Myth of Nations*, 105. See also Bradley, "Time Regained," at 15.

[269] For example, Nicholas Higham, ed. *Britons in Anglo-Saxon England* (Woodbridge: Boydell and Brewer, 2007).

[270] Martin Biddle and Birthe Kjolbye-Biddle, "The Repton Stone," *Anglo-Saxon England* 14 (1985): 233–92.

[271] Geary, *Myth of Nations*, 62.

[272] Susan Oosthuizen, *Landscapes Decoded. The Origins and Development of Cambridgeshire's Medieval Fields* (Hatfield: University of Hertfordshire Press, 2006), 52–59; Oosthuizen, *Anglo-Saxon Fenland*, 53. See also Semple, *Perceptions of the Prehistoric*, 45–48.

[273] Reynolds, "'Anglo-Saxon' and 'Anglo-Saxons'," at 414.

Chapter 4

Another Perspective

The earlier parts of this book have argued that explanations have failed in which the emergence of the English is
predicated on the arrival in England of "the Anglo-Saxons."
Chapter 2 suggested that many aspects of late fourth-century Romano-British administrative structures, institutions,
social relationships, language, economy, and material culture could still be recognized in the considerable intricacy
of the post-imperial world. Aspects of Romano-British material culture and craftsmanship, once thought to have been
almost entirely replaced by the mid-fifth century, continued
to influence one or another form of artifact to a greater or
lesser extent from one region to another. Most of the island's
population, descended from its earlier inhabitants, continued to exploit the same landscapes in much the same ways
as their ancestors had done over the preceding centuries,
their agricultural livelihoods possibly stimulated rather than
depressed by the removal of Roman taxation. Incomers from
across Europe, north Africa, and the eastern Mediterranean
were assimilated into their communities. On the other hand,
there was also significant innovation—in material culture,
whose form took on many north-west European characteristics; in the identification by the mid-sixth century of the people of England as *Angli*, who spoke a language, English, that
was dominant by the same period; and in the restructuring of
imperial administrative and territorial units in a hierarchy of
folk territories. The degree of continuity varied by region, by

level of organizational complexity, and in localized disparities between the rapidity and intensity of adaptation and innovation. Interwoven with adapting tradition, the pace, extent, and force of change and transformation were as influenced by geography, by sector, and by scale. *Romanitas* in Wales seems gradually to have evolved into a form of Britishness that absorbed the Roman legacy of territorial organization, property rights, and language. In the east, the early seventh-century kingdoms of Kent, East Anglia, and Lindsey also developed from Romano-British administrative divisions but Old English was becoming their dominant language. Chapter 3 made a case for irreconcilable flaws in models based on the supposedly superior cultural characteristics of Germanic incomers that enabled them to take advantage of a political void created by the withdrawal of imperial troops and administration.

Chapter 4 argues for holistic, multi-stranded interpretations of how Romano-Britons evolved into the English, adapting in the short-, medium-, and the long-term to sudden events and longer-lasting processes—each varying by scale, by region, and by degree of momentum—and all underpinned by underlying continuities whose evolution was almost imperceptibly slow. It experiments in particular with the concept of the *longue durée*, those elements of society and environment that evolve most gradually and thus provide a backdrop against which the causes, processes, and effects of faster-paced adjustments can more easily be discerned.

The *Longue Durée* in its Context

The great French historian Fernand Braudel published an article in 1958 that transformed the way in which historians think about the past.[274] There and subsequently he argued that, in order to understand historical change, the events and processes of each period should be set not only in the context of regional geography and culture but also in that of a much longer chronological range—what he called the *longue durée*: "history whose passage is almost imperceptible, that of man in relationship to his environment, a history in which all change is slow, a history of constant repetition, ever-recurring cycles."[275] By setting short-term events and medium-term processes against that slower-moving background, he suggested, historians might be able determine which elements were part of an unchanged, or imperceptibly changing, inheritance from the past, which traditional elements had been modified—to a greater or lesser extent—and how, and therefore (perhaps most importantly) what the major innovations were of each period under study.[276] Without the wider context of the *longue durée*, these long-term patterns of behaviour might be elusive and there could be a danger of interpreting evidence of change as contemporary innovation when it might instead be influenced by or an evolution from older traditions.

Braudel thus proposed a complex model for explaining historical change. He suggested that some change might be stimulated by short-term processes or episodic events of which some might have a dramatic short- and/or long-term influence on society, economy, or polity; the influence of others, however intense in the short-term, may have dissipated within a relatively brief period, leaving few medium- or long-term traces. The influence of yet others—whether or not their consequences were transformative—may only have been visible only across the medium or longer term. Such short-term events in the context of late antique and early medieval England might, for example, include the early fifth-century withdrawal of the Roman army and administration, or the Justinian plagues of the mid-sixth century. Medium-term influences might be exemplified by the political, social, and economic transformations across what is called the "long" eighth century, from about 650 to 850, that were led by the kingdom of Mercia, in (for example) the control of trade implied by an insistence on a standardized coinage and the imposition of tolls. Both short- and medium-term change, Braudel suggested, should be set against the *longue durée*, the slow, continuous evolution of some aspects of social, political, and/or economic life over many centuries or even millennia.

The history of the Roman church in Britain offers an illustration of an institution adapting across a *longue durée* spanning almost two millennia. There were bishops at London, York, and Lincoln by 314.[277] Christianity survived, to a greater or lesser extent, throughout the fifth and sixth centuries, long before the arrival of St. Augustine in 595. There were churches at Canterbury and Lincoln, a shrine at Verulamium (and indications of many others), active Christian communities in eastern England, and monastic centres not only in the west and north of England but possibly also in the east.[278] By the eighth century the Roman church was as dominant as it had been before 400 and is, of course, still present in Britain today. Agriculture offers a less formal example. Romano-British and late antique preferences for breeding and rearing stock persisted in early medieval pastoral husbandry. The management of flocks of sheep and herds of cattle at the sixth-century site of West Stow (Suffolk), for instance, appears to have been derived from Romano-British practices.[279] Further afield, two varieties of cultivated apple (what we would call an eating or cooking apple in contrast to crab apples) bred by Roman farmers survive into the modern period: one is Decio; the other is Annurca, still grown in Campania, in southern Italy, and mentioned by Pliny the Elder in 77–79.[280] Each has survived because, over the intervening two millennia, successive generations of farmers have gone into their orchards every seventy years or so to graft new trees onto rootstock as their older trees began to fail.

Similar models have emerged in sociology (led by Bourdieu), economics (led by Östrom) and in environmental science (led by Holling).[281] All have been the subject of critical debate, have been developed further, and stimulated the emergence of new formulations.[282] Bourdieu suggested that our fundamental attitudes to other people across a wide range of contexts—how we expect them to treat us, as well as how we expect to treat them—are transmitted from one generation to the next through a multiplicity of unspoken attitudes and preconceptions that we mostly learn through example before adulthood, in a process of acculturation he called *habitus*.[283] Social expectations about how people should behave in specific contexts are learned implicitly through example, in a process quite different from the explicit way in which, for instance, reading Latin might be taught. They distinguish between those actions that are permissible and those that are not, but because they are only rarely articulated they can be difficult to rationalize verbally. For the same reasons, they are slow to change. *Habitus* offers an explanation, for instance, for the deep indignation that travellers abroad can feel about queuing. Those who expect access to a bus or a train to depend on *when* an individual arrives at the gate will be outraged by the behaviour of those who cleave as firmly to the certainty that simply *being at* the gate is all that counts. Bourdieu's proposition thus provides an explanatory framework for the long-term perpetuation of social norms which gradually evolve from one generation to the next, and which limit the directions within which historical change might occur.

Elinor Östrom arrived at comparable conclusions in her economic analysis of the institutions that govern rights of common.[284] Whatever their cultural or chronological contexts, such institutions tend to be framed by distinctive general principles of equity between all right-holders in a shared resource: in their access to it, in the volume of the resource they can take, in the expectation of their participation in governance, in their expectations of decision-making by consensus, and in their collective oral histories of custom and practice. At the same time, such structures are sufficiently generalized to allow each groups of commoners to respond quickly and flexibly to changing local circumstance. These principles, she suggested, provide predictable, inarticulate limits to the objectives of governance, defining what must be undertaken, what may be undertaken, and what may not—in other words, they describe what Bourdieu called *habitus*. Together those characteristics minimize the risk of institutional failure and offer such institutions the potential to persist for considerable periods of time. The courts of the commons that governed the medieval and early modern fens of the Soke of Bolingbroke or the Wapentake of Elloe (both Lincolnshire), for instance, were not unique in Britain in having fifth- or sixth-century origins—an example that Braudel might have used to illustrate the *longue durée*.[285]

C. S. Holling's model of panarchy, like Braudel's *longue durée*, is structured on the proposition that the speed of social and ecological change varies at a range of scales across smaller- and larger-scale localities, communities, and collectivities, and is controlled by innumerable dynamic relationships between them as long-term traditions interact with fast or sudden changes (Figure 5). [286] Holling suggested that two kinds of stimuli are critical in creating and sustaining change and adaptation over time. On the one hand, the after-effects of small, fast changes can have a sufficient impact on larger, slower social dynamics; on the other, such changes may be ameliorated and absorbed by long-term social memory most often perpetuated in oral traditions of custom and practice.[287] Severe weather events, for instance, are short-term episodes that may have dramatic effects on the local economies within which they occur, at least in part through their ecological impact. While some communities might experience severe long-term consequences, their general effects on others may be relatively limited. The catastrophic marine floods of January 31, 1953, when the sea broke through flood defences in Holland and eastern England are an example. In the short term many hundreds of people were drowned, thousands of hectares were flooded, buildings and roads destroyed, and innumerable crops and livestock washed away; today, most communities have recovered and longer-term effects are most visible in infrastructure subsequently constructed to prevent a recurrence rather than in those local landscapes.[288]

Climate change, on the other hand, is a longer-term process whose impacts on ecological systems are likely to be felt on a much wider geographic scale and are likely to have longer-term consequences on economies and societies. The late antique shift across central southern Britain from a predominantly arable to a predominantly pastoral economy is believed to reflect a climatic downturn which seems reached

Slow changes on a large scale

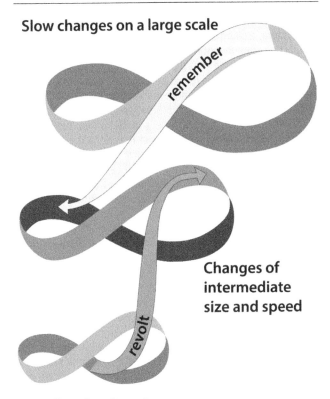

remember

Changes of
intermediate
size and speed

revolt

Small and or fast changes

Figure 5. Holling's model of panarchy models the effects of
small, fast changes on larger, slower historical processes;
the influences of changes of intermediate size and speed;
and amelioration of change by long-term remembered traditions
(© Susan Oosthuizen 2018, after Gunderson and Holling,
Panarchy, p. 26, Figure 4, with amendments).

its nadir between 450 and 550.[289] A successful social-ecological system, Holling suggested, "can invent and experiment, benefitting from inventions that create opportunity while it is kept safe from those that destabilize the system because of their nature or excessive exuberance";[290] a less successful, more rigid system will be more vulnerable to systemic shock. In this he echoes Östrom's characterizations of institutions of collective governance or Braudel's model of *habitus* in a formulation which neatly maps against Braudel's *longue durée*.

How might the application of such models to the period between 400 and 800 illuminate the processes through which the English emerged? Can the removal of imperial military and administrative oversight in the early fifth century, or the cessation of Roman coin imports, be evaluated in these terms? Were these "small and fast" changes with little long-term impact, or ones of "intermediate size and speed" that required the adaption of local institutions? How significant were changes in material culture in these terms? And, can social institutions be identified that embody Braudel's vision of the *longue durée*, Bourdieu's of *habitus*, Östrom's of structures for minimizing institutional risk, and Holling's of the "larger slower cycle" whose flexibility and generalizability facilitate renewal? If such institutions can be identified in late antique and early medieval England, perhaps they might provide a wider context against which the significance of medium- and short-term stimulus, response, and adaption might be measured and—as crucially—interpreted and explained.

The remainder of this chapter focuses on those questions through the lens of the rights of property of peasant cultivators. That choice is deliberate. Subsistence farming dominated the lives of most people between the late fourth and early eighth centuries—and for long before and long after. All aspects of that agricultural economy depended for their stability and sustainability on property rights over land, whether arable or non-arable. Everyone had an interest in the organization and management of the productive landscape, whether as owner, tenant, or labourer. A household that neglected this year to plough, sow and harvest its fields, and to manage its flocks and herds, might not survive to try again next year. Then, as now, ditches, hedges, banks, walls, and other physical boundaries embodied control over resources through agricultural property rights. They gave material expression to the social relationships, status, personal and communal identities, livelihoods and hierarchies that were built on and around the farming economy.[291] That is, they were a visual mnemonic for titles of property and their descent, individual and household wealth and status, family and community histories and genealogies, customary and mythic traditions of farming practice, the potential to generate a surplus or acquire goods, and opportunities for personal interaction with elites through tribute, gift-giving, or taxation. If there was transformative change across England between the late fourth and late eighth centuries, that cultural revolution might be expected to be reflected in adaptions to or transformations of the agricultural landscape in which access to rights of property was critical.

A Property Rights Approach: Premise, Definitions, and Proposition

Legal historians suggest that property should be conceived not as a physical entity, a "thing," but as bundles of rights that "help a man form those expectations which he can reasonably hold in his dealings with others. Those expectations find expression in the laws, customs, and mores of a society. An owner of property rights possesses the consent of fellowmen to allow him to act in particular ways" in relation to his property—for example, an object, a piece of land, an animal, or a person—provided that his actions are within the limits specified by his right.[292] A man who is the sole owner of a piece of land may manage it as he pleases provided that he does not stray beyond its boundaries and does not undertake activities that are likely to be a risk to his neighbours. While definitions of forms of property right and of the precise distinctions between them tend to be hazily delineated, two are of particular interest in the context of peasant holdings across late antique and early medieval England.[293] The first concerns what might loosely be called private rights of property: exclusively vested in an individual (or a group behaving as an individual) who has sole rights of access, exploitation, and disposition of the defined property.[294] Second, common, or shared property rights are held by exclusive groups of co-owners who share in the equitable exploitation of specified areas of (usually natural) resource like pasture, woodland, fishing waters, salt marsh, and so on.[295] They are similar to exclusive property rights in that membership of the right-holding group is exclusive; they are unlike private property rights in that common rights in a natural resource are limited rather than absolute.[296] The proposition explored below is that the continuity or discontinuity of private and/or common property rights in agricultural land between the fifth and the eighth centuries may offer an index of the degree of evolution in or disruption to peasant communities in late antique and early medieval England.

For historians, the earliest surviving documentary evidence suggests that private and common property rights were both recognized by the late fifth or early sixth centuries. The oldest surviving written English law codes—believed to have been based traditions of Romano-British customary law—take the existence of both for granted.[297] At the beginning of the seventh century, for instance, Æthelbert of Kent assumed that privately owned homesteads and estates were conventional components in the landscape of his kingdom.[298] Both private and common rights over land are assumed in the later seventh-century laws of Ine of Wessex, whose legislation included conditions limiting rights of redress to damage from stray cattle both within a *ceorl*'s homestead (*worthig*) as well as on land—whether arable or grassland—that was shared by a number of cultivators.[299]

Archaeologists straightforwardly assume the existence of both forms of property right in prehistoric and Roman Britain. Their identification of rights of private property is essentially based on morphological criteria: a single farmstead, or a tight cluster of (say) two or three farmsteads, controlling access to one or more enclosed fields is generally interpreted as an expression of private property rights. Neolithic and Bronze Age farmsteads and their fields on Dartmoor, for instance, have been interpreted as private landholdings.[300] Iron Age farmsteads and their fields, each believed to have been in the exclusive, private occupation of single family units, have been identified from Cornwall to Yorkshire and beyond.[301] A variation in the form of private property, based on limited inheritance rights over such landholdings among agnatic kin, appears to have been a prehistoric tradition that persisted into the early medieval period.[302] There seems to have been little disruption of private property rights in the Roman period.[303] Across most of rural Roman Britain traditional rights of private property appear largely to have been respected after 43, most visible in the accumulation of land into large villa estates.[304] Landscapes in which grazing was allocated to or owned by a single household or individual, have been widely identified.[305] Examples include Henllys (Gower), where access to a large pastoral enclosure was controlled by a single Romano-British farmstead, and Roystone Grange (Derbyshire) which appears to have been in the sole occupation of a single family, household or kinship group from the Neolithic into the Romano-British periods.[306] Since some Anglo-Saxon estates appear to have been the direct descendants of Roman or even prehistoric landed properties, some form of hereditary private tenure may reasonably be inferred to have existed across the first millennium.[307]

Historians place the origins of shared rights of property in the late antique period, working from the assumption that the earliest documentary evidence in the late seventh-century laws of King Ine of Wessex was also evidence of their earliest occurrence.[308] Neilson observed in 1920 that, for instance, that their "origin … goes back to the early days of [the Anglo-Saxon] settlement."[309] Later historians have continued to support that position.[310] As late as 2008, Roberts was still able to conclude that "The question is not of the presence of manors or estates in early Anglo-Saxon times, but of the *emergence* of rights in land and rights over land."[311] Yet the premise underlying that historiography is flawed. It is, of course, possible that Ine had developed a new law code for newly introduced rights of common and that the assumption is valid. The problem is that it is just as possible that the law-code simply reiterated existing custom and that concepts of shared property were already ancient by the later seventh century.

Archaeologists have consistently simply accepted the existence of prehistoric and Romano-British rights of shared property. "Empty zones"—areas of long-standing non-arable usage, devoid of almost any archaeological evidence, and usually separated by earthwork boundaries from contemporary fields and settlements—are conventionally described as areas exploited under shared or common rights.[312] Such areas demonstrate some distinctive characteristics: routes into them tended to be accessible by all households in a settlement, or by a number of settlements; and they were not subdivided into smaller units that might indicate their apportionment between farms or households. Herring, for instance, has suggested that Bronze Age pastures on Bodmin Moor in Cornwall "were probably subject to [collective] controls on livestock numbers and against trespassers."[313] Similar prehistoric landscapes have been identified from Devon to the Cheviots and the Yorkshire Wolds, across the chalk downs of southern England, on marsh, fen, and floodplain from Somerset Levels and the East Anglian fens and along the major English rivers, as well as on clay plateaux from the Cotswolds to Northamptonshire and Suffolk.[314]

There is, however, some debate among archaeologists about the persistence of shared rights of property after 43. Millett, for example, has argued that such collective rights might already have become more restricted before the Roman invasion.[315] Gerrard has recently taken that proposition further, suggesting that all rights of collective property were eliminated in Britain after the Roman conquest by the imposition of Roman law whose consequence was a complete re-allocation of rural property rights.[316] Roman imperial administrators, he argues, treated all land—including commons—as private property. Nonetheless, the weight of scholarly opinion takes an opposing view.[317] Most agree that imperial law in the Roman provinces provided a normative, flexible framework within which customary forms of property rights could be managed and incrementally adapted—a question of doing things in traditionally accepted, expected ways rather than imposing an entirely new set of formal rules. Stevens suggested that "it was Roman practice not to force its own laws on its subjects";[318] Winkler has concurred, speaking for most in suggesting that "the legitimacy of local [prehistoric] custom" including that governing rights in property "was recognised in Roman imperial constitutions."[319] That is, it seems most likely that all prehistoric property rights, including common rights, persisted and continued to be governed through the Roman period under long-standing prehistoric customary traditions influenced by Roman law, itself "more adaptable and less absolute than was traditionally thought."[320] That conclusion is supported by the apparent assumptions of the seventh-century laws cited at the beginning of this section.

The proposition explored below is that the continuity or discontinuity of property rights in agricultural land between the fifth and the eighth centuries may offer an index of the degree of evolution in or disruption to peasant communities in late antique and early medieval England. It begins by examining the evidence for that persistence, or lack of it, in the landscape.

Continuity or Disruption of Property Rights in England, ca. 400–800: The Evidence of the Agricultural Landscape

It should be said at the outset that there are many places in which prehistoric and Romano-British fields were abandoned by their cultivators in the fifth or sixth centuries. In some places, even where patchy hedgerows or the earthworks of silted-up ditches or degraded banks survived, new boundaries were laid out along quite different alignments when ownership was once more extended over these areas. On Salisbury Plain in Wiltshire, for example, at least some prehistoric and Romano-British field boundaries had become sufficiently faint on the ground or irrelevant in local tradition to be ignored by seventh-century tithing boundaries.[321] Middle or late Anglo-Saxon fields were laid out across the deserted remains of earlier landscapes from Wiltshire, Hampshire, Berkshire, Cambridgeshire, Essex, Northamptonshire, and Nottinghamshire, to Derbyshire and beyond.[322] In other cases, even where the ridges of medieval cultivation fit into "the framework of much older lynchets that had fossilized patterns of Roman fields modifying prehistoric ones"—as at West Chisenbury and Fyfield Down (both Wiltshire)—it is impossible to say whether they were continuously ploughed or whether husbandmen, reoccupying an abandoned landscape, simply re-used existing boundaries that they could see on the ground.[323]

There are, however, now so many more examples of the persistence of prehistoric and Romano-British field layouts into and beyond the early Anglo-Saxon centuries that continuity of the occupation of farm land across the fifth and sixth centuries is almost certainly the norm rather than the exception.[324] Examples include the "grid of ditched paddocks or closes" of a Roman villa estate at Barton Court (Oxfordshire) framed the Anglo-Saxon settlement there;[325] a middle Anglo-Saxon settlement at Catholme (Staffordshire) lying on "a parcel of Romano-British farmland";[326] while Romano-British fields at Church Down and Catherington in Chalton (Hampshire), Mucking and Havering (Essex), Bow Brickhill (Buckinghamshire), Sutton Courtenay (Berkshire), and Yarnton (Oxfordshire) continued to be cultivated into the seventh century.[327] Many were in continuous use for long enough to be used as the framework for medieval open-field landscapes. "Part of a system older than the common fields, into which the furlongs were fitted and from which the layout of the common fields emerged" survived at Castle Ashby, Haddon, Orton Longueville, Elton and Warmington (Northamptonshire), and similar instances have been found from Wiltshire to Herefordshire and Staffordshire; across the midlands from Oxford to Leicestershire, Cambridgeshire, and Lincolnshire;

and from Sussex to Yorkshire, across Buckinghamshire, Hertfordshire, Norfolk, and Suffolk.[328] The archaeological evidence indicates relatively little visible change in the alignments, layouts and boundaries of fields small enough to indicate private property rights. Whatever the details of their cropping, the same hedges, ditches, banks, and walls continued to define the rights of property held over them. That continuity might indicate that there was little dislocation over those centuries in definitions of who was entitled to rights of property, in the structure or governance of land ownership, and how those rights were given physical form in the landscape.

That problem of the identification of continuity might be approached from another direction by asking what one might expect to see in the landscape if private property rights had been disrupted by immigration from north-west Europe or the replacement of Romano-British by Germanic elites. There are at least four possibilities. The first case takes the example of incomers from a quite different cultural background who arrive in such numbers that they rapidly displace or achieve dominance over existing communities, confiscating and redistributing their land among the new colonists. In that case, one might expect to find new conceptualizations of property right and/or new structures for their allocation in the landscape expressed in the destruction of existing field layouts and their replacement by new landscapes with a quite different morphology and on quite different alignments. For example, Flemish colonists brought in by the Norman kings to subdue south Wales were settled on land confiscated from its existing Welsh owners; the incomers laid out new settlements on different alignments and with different morphologies like the property boundaries of their new town of Templeton (Pembrokeshire) which overlie and cut across the grain of the older fieldscape still visible beneath them.[329] There is no evidence of similar changes in the late antique or early medieval English fieldscape.

A second possibility is suggested where incomers settled alongside or at a distance from existing communities, without assimilation or integration between the two, resulting in two quite different sets of alignments and morphological forms lying alongside each other. Byzantine Constantinople, for instance, perpetuated the grid plan of the late Roman city from which it evolved; new suburbs that grew up after the Ottoman conquest of 1453, however, are organic, unplanned and irregular in layout.[330] Similar examples can be seen across southern Spain, where planned later medieval urban extensions lie alongside the irregular lanes of the older Moorish cities like Cordoba, Granada and Malaga conquered by Ferdinand and Isabella of Castile in the later fifteenth century. There is no evidence of such contrasting morphologies and layouts in the late antique or early medieval English fieldscape.

A third case is exemplified in the example of around one hundred and fifty thousand Jewish refugees from persecution in the Russian empire who fled to Britain over a few decades between the late nineteenth and early twentieth centuries, many settling initially in the east end of London. Comparison of a map showing the intensity of their settlement in the streets around Petticoat Lane in 1899 with another of the same area in 1827 shows almost no change between the two dates in the underlying geography of property boundaries in the area suggesting that the newcomers were assimilated into existing institutional structures.[331]

Useful though they are in stimulating us to think about what may actually have happened on the ground in early medieval England, each of these scenarios has an important, inherent weakness: changes in private property rights may not necessarily offer a reliable index of the kind of social transformation we seek. Property held exclusively by an individual is vulnerable to idiosyncratic change. The persistence, removal, or adjustment of its boundaries may simply be the result of unpredictable, idiosyncratic influences such as death, gift, marriage, sale, or a ruler's or owner's whim. That weakness is exemplified, too, in a fourth case in which existing communities are entirely displaced and replaced by incomers who simply adopt their homesteads and field systems wholesale, leaving the landscape unchanged. An example of the latter can be found in the forcible expulsion of the inhabitants of Great and Little Childerley, and Wimpole (all Cambridgeshire) by the early sixteenth and later seventeenth centuries respectively to make way for private parks and formal gardens.[332] Perhaps continuity of rights of private property cannot be recognized in agricultural landscapes without more intensive research and, at least currently, have little to tell us about the emergence of the English. Shared property rights—rights of common—may offer a more useful approach.

Agricultural Land Exploited Under Shared Rights of Property

Could there be long-term continuities in areas exploited under shared rights of property from (say) prehistoric or Roman Britain into pre-Conquest England? Palaeoenvironmental, archaeological, place-name, and documentary evidence each suggest the possibility.

The wide geographical scale of palaeoenvironmental evidence from commons shared between a number of right-holders implies their continuous use for collective grazing over centuries and, sometimes, millennia. Across much of Bodmin Moor, in south-west Britain, "the vegetation of the moor seems to have been very similar [from the Iron Age] throughout the first millennium AD, with predominantly pastoral land use, plus some grassland management for hay."[333] The similarly extensive persistence of specific mosaics of "high quality, species-rich grassland" on the extensive commons of the Cheviot Hills of Northumberland remained relatively unchanged from the late Iron Age until the mid-eighteenth century—something that could only be achieved by deliberate collective management.[334] Comparable pollen evidence indicates continuous histories of grazing under shared property rights, too, on the uplands of Exmoor and Dartmoor, on marsh in the Somerset Levels and in the East Anglian fens, at Chalton (Hampshire) and other parts of the chalk downs of southern England, at Minchinhampton (Gloucestershire) and other places on clay plateaus of the Cotswolds, at Newbottle and other locations in Northamptonshire, and from Suffolk to the Yorkshire Wolds.[335]

The persistence of the boundaries of commons across the *longue durée* can often be identified from distinctive physical characteristics, including substantial earthworks to define their boundaries; collective management and grazing of large areas indicated by the absence of their subdivision into smaller units that record their apportionment between households; and equitable access to them from all the farmsteads and settlements in the vicinity.[336] Many also demonstrate evidence—from prehistory into medieval period and after—of substantial gatherings of large groups of people in periods when the herds were arriving or departing, and when disputes about rights to grazing, ownership of stock, and damage to animals were most likely to occur.[337]

In other places, long-term continuity of collectively exploited commons from the Roman into the post-Roman centuries is indicated by the survival of all or part of their Brittonic names into the medieval period. They include Penge (*pen*, "high" and *cēt*, "wood") (Kent), Barnwood (*bryn* "wood") and Maisemore (*maes*, "plain" and *mor*, "moor") (both Gloucestershire), *coit maur* ("great wood," now called Selwood) (Wiltshire), *Letocetum*, a large Roman wood south of Lichfield (Staffordshire), the Forest of Wyre (Worcestershire), woods around Bunbury and Malpas (both Cheshire), and so on.[338] The county name for Somerset (*sumor*, "summer" and *saete*, "peoples with a Romano-British identity") records the seasonal movement of animals to and from the Somerset Levels; *Andredswald*, the Old English name for the Weald, in which all the freemen of Kent and Sussex had ancient rights of common, was derived from *Anderita*, the Roman name for Pevensey.[339] Jones argued that woods along the boundaries of *Burghshire* (a large early medieval estate focused on Aldborough (Yorkshire) had been continuously exploited under rights of common from prehistory into the middle ages.[340] There is little sign in any of these landscapes of any break in their exploitation in the fifth or sixth centuries.

That conclusion might be explored from another perspective by asking what physical or archaeological evidence might be expected if there had been disruption of exploitation of an area under common rights. There are two possibilities under which no evidence might be expected to have been created: the instant transfer of all rights of common to outsiders who displaced a local group of commoners; or the complete cessation of the exploitation of a common under rights of shared property for long enough for all memory of their character, limits, governance, and management to disappear, and the coincidental re-introduction of common rights over the same area.

The first case—the replacement within a short period of time of all local holders of shared rights in a common by newcomers—is a particularly complicated explanation where there is no evidence of abandonment of the land. It requires the transfer, within a brief period and without interruption to the governance and management of the common, of all existing common rights in it to a set of individuals who were entirely ignorant of its workings and history. The success of such a transfer depends on the efficient transmission from the original group to its successors within a short length of time of all existing institutional knowledge, built up over a long period and held in oral traditions of custom and practice, including such key practical elements as the finer detail of territorial boundaries and the subtle knowledge of local soils, topography, drainage, and growing conditions required for the productive, sustainable, day-to-day management of the common. In a relatively unstructured, pre-literate political environment where institutional support for such arrangements was lacking, the successful transfer of such complex bodies of knowledge seems unlikely and one might expect to see evidence of some ecological disruption to the management of the grazing.

The second case requires as complex an explanation. In order for the break between the two distinct periods of usage to be complete, all recollection of the earlier common would have to be lost, a condition whose success would depend on the interruption of commoning for at least one generation and almost certainly longer. The location and boundaries of the common would need to be forgotten, as well as knowledge of soil, drainage, and grasses that underpin detailed arrangements for its successful management and regulation, and the achievement of appropriate levels of productivity. A break in usage of at least a generation would be long enough to be visible in archaeological and/or palynological evidence: for example, if the common were divided into fields and paddocks, or if it reverted to dense woodland (which Rackham suggests would occur within thirty years—a generation).[341] The case also requires the coincidence that two unconnected groups treat precisely the same area as a common resource in two distinct periods. A substantial change in ownership of shared property rights might reasonably be expected to be visible either in the landscape itself or in the palynological evidence. And such evidence is only rarely found.

A further problem is the universality of definitions of common rights across the early medieval British Isles. Early medieval property rights across the islands comprised two inseparable components: shared rights to the natural resources of the district *and* an arable holding sufficient to maintain an extended household.[342] Every *bonheddig* (freeman) in early medieval Wales, for instance, had a right to common grazing on the pastures of his clan, just as, in seventh- and eighth-century Ireland (and, perhaps, long before) common land was held by the kin group—*túath*—such that incursions on it by strangers were offences against the group as a whole, and every freeman within the *túath* had a right to share in its exploitation.[343] In England, the intrinsic connection between rights of common and ancient tenements are held to have their origins in fifth- and sixth-century polities that were sometimes referred to as *folcland*—territories controlled by the 'folk' who held property rights in them.[344] Rights of common in non-arable resources were a potent symbol not only of membership of a polity, but also of each right-holder's free status and the concomitant public rights and responsibilities through which his social standing was displayed.[345] Their existence across the British Isles in such an early period indicates that they cannot necessarily be ascribed to a break between late Roman and early medieval rights of property, or the introduction of new forms of shared property as a consequence of a supposed *adventus*. They are found not only in eastern and south-eastern England where "the Anglo-Saxons" are said to have settled, but also in the north and west of Britain which they never colonized. Instead, the documentary, palaeoenvironmental, archaeological, and place-name evidence each suggests long-standing continuities of shared exploitation from prehistory into the early medieval period, from which the persistent recognition of common property rights over areas of natural resource over similarly long periods can be inferred. The possibility is vividly illustrated in traditional practice. The collective management of woodland to produce standardized timber for houses and large constructions, poles of uniform diameter for fencing and hurdling, and underwood for brushwood has been practised since the Neolithic.[346] The Sweet Track in the Somerset Levels, for example, was constructed in a single year in the fifth or fourth millennium BCE by two communities, working from opposite sides of the marsh, each drawing on separate stands of managed woodland and coppice; later similar prehistoric, Romano-British and medieval causeways have been found across the wetlands of the Somerset Levels and of the Cambridgeshire fenland, using timber, hurdles, poles, and brushwood from managed resources in various combinations.[347] The materials used in a middle Iron Age house on the Glastonbury fens included oak coppice cut on a ten- to fifteen-year cycle, hazel or willow coppice cut on a four- to four-year cycle, seventeen thousand bundles of reeds and eight cubic metres of clay.[348] Ancient managed woodland, perhaps at one time belonging to nearby Iron Age and Romano-British settlements, has been identified at Knook Down East (Wiltshire) and at Rayleigh (Essex).[349] The social hierarchy and relationships that characterized the Romano-British peasant households that farmed these landscapes may also have persisted into the fifth and sixth centuries. Their farmhouses continued to be built on the same rectangular plans that had become traditional across Britain from the first century of the current era, "an expression of a peasant family/household unit" whose economy and social traditions were little changed by the withdrawal of Roman administration in the early fifth century.[350]

General continuity over the *longue durée* of structures for the governance and management of commons seems likely unless we are to postulate both the complete desertion of large tracts of countryside and a duration for that abandonment for a period long enough to allow all norms governing their past use and management to disappear from living memory. There is, as argued above, little evidence that this occurred on any wide scale. Daily, monthly, and seasonal agricultural tasks relating to stock made a fundamental contribution to subsistence in all periods. A man who lost his herds or flocks, or the pastures to which he was accustomed to take them, might (if he were able to replace either) be expected to bring his past experience and that of his neighbours and peers, maintained in oral traditions of customary practice, to his conceptions (*habitus*) of the norms, practices, and sanctions governing his future access to grazing. They suggest the long-term continuity within local communities of structures for the management of common resources.

An Institution Across the *Longue Durée*?

By the time the earliest documents were written the same criteria for access to common rights were found across Britain: they were limited to those who were both members of a polity and who held free status. The universality across the British Isles in the earliest documentary records of criteria for allowing access to shared property rights, for the interpretation of those rights, and the forms of their governance, suggests that this form of land-holding was already very old by 600. They were found in all areas of Britain, irrespective of their many different histories across the first millennium of the current era, and of variations in regional geographies, cultures, economies, social hierarchies, and even languages. Changes to land held under shared property rights tend to be considerably more conservative and may, perhaps, be more likely to provide evidence of long-term adaptive institutional continuity that Braudel might have had in mind in describing his vision of the *longue durée*. Commons, property rights in them, and the institutions through which they are governed tend to be "enduring, selective, and stable in membership, conferring specific rights and duties, owning wealth as a group, administering discipline, having goals, being clearly identifiable as a group."[351] They are predisposed to incremental adaptation to change and thus to longevity.[352]

Rights of common brought with them participation in collective governance and legal responsibilities exercised across the polity as a whole that offered a minimum social position, however ill-defined, to landholders whose status and identity was based at least in part on their access to those rights. The public legal obligations that they were required to render to the territory as a whole were substantial marks of status: the expectation of participation in collective governance at all levels, membership of a communal militia, and contributions of characteristic public renders, services, and money payments. Faith has emphasized the degree to which "the idea of "law-worthiness," of entitlement to participate in the system, was of paramount importance to personal status" in early medieval England.[353] They also offered all free landholders the opportunity to connect with political leaders and their elites through reciprocal gift-giving, and renders in kind and in labour, and in which their own status was recognized and affirmed. Reynolds has suggested that it is not surprising that such polities were so often rationalized in terms of "communities of common descent": their mutual obligations, responsibilities, and rights, and their shared oral traditions of custom and practice, echo those between kin.[354]

An intrinsic relationship between the collective governance of natural resources belonging to entire territories and the polities that gradually evolved into the early medieval kingdoms was proposed by Neilson as long ago as 1920. She suggested that the identity of late antique and early medieval polities was not focused on the leadership of individual kings or dynasties, but drawn from the landscape they inhabited and the shared property rights that they exerted over it.

This was a complex expression of territoriality. Rights of common brought together definitions of a territory—the shared resources of a bounded political unit, with conceptions of status—the restriction of rights of common to free men, with a belief (real or imagined) that the group was also linked by kinship, with an expectation that those with common rights were also participants in its governance.[355] Wychwood, the wood of the *Hwicce*, had been subdivided by the late seventh-century;[356] Sherwood was the *scir wuda*, the wood of the shire administered from Nottingham;[357] and rights of common in Dartmoor attached to free holdings across Devon were first documented by the mid-eighth century but may have had prehistoric origins.[358] Neilson's identification of clusters of vills each sharing rights of common in discrete areas of the early medieval fenland is widely accepted, more recently identified with the geography of late seventh-century polities, all persisting into the early modern period, and many offering some evidence of prehistoric origins.[359] All were governed by regular assemblies in which all right-holders were expected to participate, in which each had an equal voice, in which decisions were made by consensus, and whose decisions were recorded in oral histories of custom and practice.

Neilson's work remains unchallenged. Davies and Vierck wrote over half a century later that "it is groups and associations of people that form the raw material of early political development, not the carving up of territory."[360] Fowler described in 2002 how for "much of the [first millennium AD] it seems that pasture was defined as much by the right to feed animals over certain areas of land as by definitions of land itself";[361] and Roberts asserted in 2008—just twelve years short of a century after Neilson's work on Lincolnshire was first published—that "at first [commons] were shared by the whole territory of the shire, but were gradually appropriated to individual parishes or townships."[362]

Late antique and early medieval polities and their sub-regions have been identified across Britain from territorial rights of common to which freemen in each of their communities were entitled.[363] Studies in Kent, in the east Anglian fenland

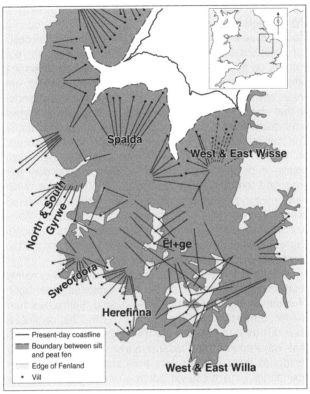

Figure 6. The medieval rights of common in the East Anglian fenland of discrete groups of contiguous vills, each focused on an exclusive area of fen grazing, preserve the geography of fifth- and sixth-century 'folk' territories—whose names were recorded in the late seventh century (© Susan Oosthuizen 2017).

and on the Yorkshire Wolds—areas of supposed early Germanic settlement and dominance—have demonstrated those continuities on a wider geographic, social, and economic scale across a *longue durée* that begins in prehistory and extends into the middle ages and later.[364] Similar results have been identified in areas far beyond that region, most notably in the Cheviots, on Salisbury Plain, on Dartmoor, and Bodmin Moor.[365] In all weathers, in all social circumstances, in all political conditions, the day-to-day preoccupation of most men was focused on how to generate a sufficient volume of food and other goods to support their households from one day, one week, one month, and one year to the next. A lack of attention to that objective could be disastrous in an economy in which a minimum level of subsistence had to be produced at home. The stability and long-term maintenance of the environment on which their pastoral husbandry—and thus their livelihoods—depended was a critical factor in framing their personal and territorial identities and social relationships. While early medieval men and women lived within complicated, changing hierarchies of dominant and subordinate polities, principalities, and kingdoms their territorial names frequently expressed what they regarded as most important: a collective identity drawn from the landscapes they occupied.

In fenland, for instance, late seventh-century polities named themselves from the landscapes they exploited under rights of common (Figure 6). The *Gyrwe* named themselves from the fen; the *Spaldingas* from the river Welland that dominated their territory; the *Sweord ora* from a long narrow peninsula that led deep into their extensive wetland grazing.[366] Those territories were adapted into pre-Conquest administrative boundaries, into medieval administrative boundaries, and into those of the modern era, demonstrating a remarkable persistence over at least 1500 years. At least some of those territories, their commons, and the institutions through which they were collectively governed, may have had Romano-British or even prehistoric origins.[367] That continuity of aspects of territory, property right, economy, and society suggests that most political change was either very short-lived and/or adaptive and evolutionary, rather than characterized by any sudden revolutionary transformation. Indeed, harnessing traditional structures of collective governance to political expression in the assemblies of emergent late antique kingdoms may have given the political leaders of the fifth, sixth, and seventh centuries another kind of opportunity to "dress up as [what they thought of as] Romans" whether or not the tradition was in fact "Roman."[368]

The possibility that rights of common over natural resources may have had sufficient longevity to place them in Braudel's *longue durée* or among Holling's "large and slow" social institutions is indicated by their characteristics: they are legal rights, enforceable by sanction; there is restricted access to such rights; and there is equity among right-holders in all aspects of the governance, regulation, and exploitation of the common.[369] By reserving governance of local day-to-day issues of resource allocation, regulation, and management to regular assemblies of individual groups of right-holders, the flexibility and responsiveness of broader principles of collective governance offers the potential for institutions governing commons to meet their underlying objectives continuously over long periods of time.[370] Structured for survival and adaptability across the *longue durée*, commons offer a good example of "systems of social behavior which provide a framework within which the individual can operate, safeguarding on the one hand the structure of the community, and thus its power to reproduce itself, while providing the individual with carefully circumscribed opportunities to engage in competitive display."[371]

Institutions for managing the agricultural economy through rights of common property required the persistence over long periods of time of collective traditions of custom and practice in the structures of social relations, identity, territoriality, and governance. It satisfies Braudel's formulation of a *longue durée* that provides a backcloth against with the continuities within, and the innovations of, short- and medium-term change can be assessed across the four centuries after the withdrawal of the Roman army and administration from Britain in a formulation that does not depend on cultural stereotypes.

Conclusions

Chapters 2 and 3 argued that the opposition of "Romano-British" versus "Anglo-Saxon" communities offers a false dichotomy. There is little evidence of any early medieval social restructuring in which "Anglo-Saxon" migrant elites reduced existing "Romano-British" communities to servile status. Instead, continuity of agricultural exploitation and the invisibility of differences in or between communities in terms of their political structure, the languages they spoke, or their material culture, suggests that local groups continued to occupy land their ancestors had held, and that incomers, whether small or large in number, were by and large assimilated. Late Spoken Latin place-names—especially in those areas believed to have been colonized by "the Anglo-Saxons"—indicate a level of administrative continuity for some Romano-British political territories; others may have been entirely new. Some were long-lived, others less permanent. There is, however, no evidence to suggest a political takeover by "Anglo-Saxons" of existing communities, or of the foundation of new, different "Germanic" kingdoms by immigrant elites. Nor does the vividly apparent change in the material culture of the period indicate demographic, cultural, or social upheaval. Most early medieval households used the same goods, lived in the same kinds of houses, farmed the same kinds of fields, and drove their cattle to the same shared pastures. It is impossible to distinguish between them in terms of their cultural background. This is not to argue that there was never displacement or conquest of one population by another; it is to argue that continuity should be assumed unless there is clear evidence—lacking here—to the contrary.

Chapter 4 has argued that the intersecting complexities of long-, medium-, and short-term change in models developed by Braudel, Bourdieu, Östrom, and Holling offer a framework for exploring that history. Long-term traditions provided a foil and a context for the short- and medium-term events and processes, adaptions, innovations, and transformations of the post-imperial centuries. Change across the medium term is most visible in the adaptation in the fifth and sixth centuries of Roman structures for administering localities, the judiciary, armies, and the church; and in the continued development of the languages of Roman-Britain—Brittonic and Late

Spoken Latin—for conducting that business. Initially spoken alongside Old English those languages were eventually dominated by it although bilingualism—perhaps even multilingualism—was common until at least the ninth century, even in eastern England. In the early fifth-century those changes are most visible in preferences for goods that came from the areas bordering onto the North Sea beyond the Roman Empire, rather than those from the Mediterranean. The introduction and evolution of cruciform brooches offers an illustrative example.[372] The earliest cruciform brooches appear to have been imports, brought into Britain in the early decades of the fifth century. They became increasingly popular from the late fifth century and the form was reproduced by local craftsmen working in Romano-British traditions. Eventually over the sixth and early seventh centuries they evolved into more complicated, better designed, and increasingly expensive forms.[373] That later development, stimulated by imports, of Romano-British technology, craftsmanship, and design occurred in the political and administrative context of (mostly) small-scale territories in which late antique distinctions of social identity and status continued to evolve. In the early to middle sixth century the brooches were increasingly used alongside distinctive forms of dress to signal wealth and status among adult, especially older, women in each household, and may initially also have signaled regional differences.[374] The distinctions in Ine's laws, discussed in chapter 3 above, between late Roman and early medieval status and forms of landholding illuminates that context. By the early seventh century, cruciform brooches were worn across central and southern England, from Rutland in the north to Kent in the south, and as far west as Gloucestershire.[375] The choice of particular forms of material culture, rather than an index of immigrant ethnicity, may simply have reflected the expression of one or another aspect of a contemporary, and developing, identity.[376]

Figure 7 demonstrates that conjectural model in diagrammatic form. Slow change across the *longue durée* is represented by common property rights, their collective governance and the social relations they embody; by long-term continuities in the agricultural economy whose interruption would be catastrophic; and by assumptions—*habitus*—of culture and social behaviour implicit in fifth-century conceptions of what it meant to be Roman (*Romanitas*), in the Late Spoken Latin that many continued to speak into the eighth century; and in traditional craft skills and aesthetics. Examples of events likely to have small, fast effects might include the withdrawal of the Roman army and administration in the early fifth century, the Justinian plagues of the mid-sixth century, and attacks from Picts, Scots, and Saxons. Climate change was a medium-term change, taking place over several centuries. Each contributed to the evolution of military structures, the continued development of social hierarchies, and the emergence of territorial units, including kingdoms; to changes in the expression of personal identity and status; and to changes in the character of material culture.

Moving away from what Gildas and Bede and the court singers wanted us to think, and what unfounded preconceptions and premises might direct us to believe, the emergence of the English should be sought among prehistoric communities and territories that had developed through the period of Roman control and into the post-imperial decades and centuries that followed. Almost all the fifth-century men and women who used these new forms of material culture, and who spoke English as a second (or third) language, traced their ancestry into the prehistoric and Romano-British past and made their livings in much the same ways as their predecessors. They found no conflict in continuing also to speak Brittonic and Late Spoken Latin, in living within administrative areas whose boundaries had been established in the first century CE or before, in turning for their defence to legal and military structures explicitly modelled on Roman antecedents, and in legitimating political authority in terms of its real or imagined Roman heritage. The long-term maintenance of the environment on which their livelihoods depended was a critical factor in underpinning the agricultural economy, and in sustaining personal and territorial identities and social relationships.

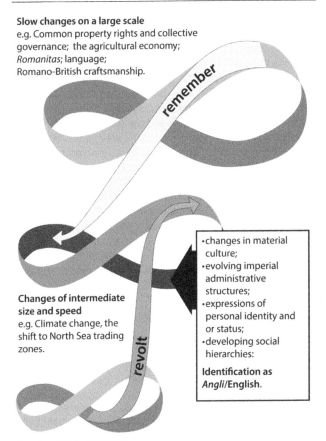

Slow changes on a large scale
e.g. Common property rights and collective
governance; the agricultural economy;
Romanitas; language;
Romano-British craftsmanship.

remember

**Changes of intermediate
size and speed**
e.g. Climate change, the
shift to North Sea trading
zones.

revolt

- changes in material
  culture;
- evolving imperial
  administrative
  structures;
- expressions of
  personal identity and
  or status;
- developing social
  hierarchies:

**Identification as
Angli/English.**

Small and/or fast changes
e.g. Withdrawal of Roman administration;
attacks by Picts, Scots and Saxons; Justinian plague.

Figure 7. An alternative model for post-Roman change: continuities
across the *longue durée* intersect over the medium term
with new/adaptive forms of social, political and cultural expression,
sometimes influenced by small, fast events of variable intensity
(© Susan Oosthuizen 2018, after Gunderson and Holling,
Panarchy, p. 26, Figure 4, with additions).

That economic stability mirrored demographic continuities. Local communities lived within a complicated, changing hierarchy of dominant and subordinate polities, principalities, and kingdoms whose names frequently expressed collective identities drawn from the landscapes they occupied, and among whom continuity may have been as commonplace as transformation. The remarkable continuity across the *longue durée* between the early fifth and the seventeenth centuries in the ecology and geography of many areas exploited under rights of common property—themselves derived from territorial institutions—suggests that most political change was either short-lived and/or adaptive and evolutionary, rather than characterized by any sudden revolutionary transformation. That rich and complex history reveals a traditional society assimilating newcomers, and continually evolving, adapting, and innovating in response to individual and collective actions, to events, small- or large-scale, sudden or expected, and to local, regional, and international influences and processes, new or familiar, rapid or slow.

Notes

[274] Fernand Braudel, "*Histoire et Sciences Sociales: La Longue Durée*," *Annales. Économies, Sociétés, Civilisations* 13, 4 (1958): 725–53. An abridged English translation was published as "History and the Social Sciences: The Long Duration," *American Behavioural Scientist* 3, 6 (1960): 3–13. A full English translation was published as "History and the Social Sciences: The *Longue Durée*," in *The* Longue Durée *and World-Systems Analysis*, ed. Richard E. Lee (Albany: State University of New York Press, 2012), 241–76.

[275] Fernand Braudel, *The Mediterranean and the Mediterranean World in the Age of Philip II*, 2 vols. (London: Collins, 1972), 1:20–21.

[276] Fernand Braudel, *The Structures of Everyday Life* (London: Collins, 1981), 560, my addition. Fernand Braudel, *On History* (Chicago: University of Chicago Press, 1982); Fernand Braudel, *The Identity of France, 1. History and Environment* (London: Fontana, 1989).

[277] F. Haverfield, "Early British Christianity," *English Historical Review* 11, 43 (1896): 417–20 and 422–25 and 427–30, at 419.

[278] For St. Martin's, Canterbury, see http://www.pastscape.org.

uk/hob.aspx?hob_id=464348; for St. Paul in the Bail, Lincoln, see https://www.pastscape.org.uk/hob.aspx?hob_id=326619; for continuity in western Britain see Richard Morris, *Churches in the Landscape* (London: Dent, 1989), 99.

[279] Pam Crabtree, *West Stow, Suffolk: Anglo-Saxon Animal Husbandry*, EAA, 47 (Colchester: East Anglian Archaeology, 1989), 212, my additions.

[280] Gaius Pliny, *Natural History: A Selection* (London: Penguin, 2004); Professor John Parker, Director of the Cambridge University Botanic Garden 1996–2010, personal communication. F. Grassi, G. Morico, and A. Sartori, "*Malus* and *Pyrus* Germplasm in Italy," in *Report of a Working Group on Malus/Pyrus*, ed. L. Maggioni, R. Janes, A. Hayes, et al. (Rome: European Cooperative Programme for Crop Genetic Resources Network, 1998), 58–65, at 58.

[281] Pierre Bourdieu, *A Theory of Practice* (Cambridge: Cambridge University Press, 1977); Elinor Östrom, *Governing the Commons. The Evolution of Institutions for Collective Action* (Cambridge: Cambridge University Press, 1990); C. S. Holling, "Understanding the Complexity of Economic, Ecological and Social Systems," *Ecosystems* 4, 5 (2001): 390–405; Lance Gunderson and C. S. Holling ed., *Panarchy. Understanding Transformations in Human and Natural Systems* (Washington, DC: Island, 2002).

[282] For structuration see Anthony Giddens, *The Constitution of Society* (London: Polity, 1984). For agency see M.-A. Dobres and John Robb, "'Doing' Agency: Introductory Remarks on Methodology," *Journal of Archaeological Method and Theory* 12, 3 (2005): 159–66; John Robb, "Beyond Agency," *World Archaeology* 42, 4 (2010): 493–520. For world systems theory see Immanual Wallerstein, *World-Systems Analysis: An Introduction* (Durham: Duke University Press, 2004). For resilience theory, see Fikret Berkes, Johan Colding, and Carl Folke, ed., *Navigating Social-Ecological Systems: Building Resilience for Complexity and Change* (Cambridge: Cambridge University Press, 2003); C. Folke, "Resilience: The Emergence of a Perspective for Social-ecological Systems Analysis," *Global Environmental Change* 16 (2006): 253–67; T. Plielinger and C. Bieling, ed., *Resilience and the Cultural Landscape* (Cambridge: Cambridge University Press, 2012). For complexity theory, see David Byrne and Gill Callaghan, *Complexity Theory and the Social Sciences: The State of the Art* (London: Routledge, 2014). For critical evaluations of these and others by archaeologists, see pt. 3, "Agency, Meaning and Practice," in *Contemporary Archaeology in Theory: The New Pragmatism*, ed. W. Preucel and S. Mrozowski (Oxford: Wiley/

Blackwell, 2010), 129–216; Michael Galaty, "World-systems Analysis and Anthropology: A New Détente?," *Reviews in Anthropology* 40 (2011): 3–26; C. M. Barton, "Complexity, Social Complexity, and Modeling," *Journal of Archaeological Method and Theory* 21 (2014): 306–24; Daniel Rogers, "Dynamic Trajectories, Adaptive Cycles, and Complexity in Culture Change," *Journal of Archaeological Method and Theory* 24 (2017): 1326–55. For collective action, see David Carballo, P. Roscoe, and Gary Feinman, "Cooperation and Collective Action in the Cultural Evolution of Complex Societies," *Journal of Archaeological Method and Theory* 21 (2014): 98–133; and David Carballo, ed. *Cooperation and Collective Action* (Boulder: University Press of Colorado, 2013).

[283] Bourdieu, *Theory of Practice*; Robb, "Beyond Agency."

[284] Östrom, *Governing the Commons*, 88–101.

[285] Neilson, *Terrier of Fleet*, xv–xviii; Oosthuizen, *The Anglo-Saxon Fenland*, 56–57; Joan Thirsk, *English Peasant Farming: The Agrarian History of Lincolnshire from Tudor to Recent Times* (London: Routledge, 2005), 29–36.

[286] Holling, "Understanding the Complexity"; Gunderson and Holling, *Panarchy*.

[287] Gunderson and Holling, *Panarchy*, 26.

[288] P. Baxter, "The East Coast Big Flood, 31 January–1 February 1953: A Summary of the Human Disaster," *Philosophical Transactions of the Royal Society* 363, 1831 (2005): 1293–1312. http://rsta.royalsocietypublishing.org/content/363/1831/1293.full, accessed June 30, 2016.

[289] Ulf Büntgen, Willy Tegel, Kurt Nicolussi, et al., "2500 Years of European Climate Variability and Human Susceptibility," *Science* 331 (February 4, 2011): 578–82, at 581; see also S. Payne, "New Insights into Climate History," *British Archaeology* 92 (2007): 54.

[290] Holling, "Understanding the Complexity," at 399; see also Gunderson and Holling, *Panarchy*.

[291] Timothy Earle, "Archaeology, Property and Prehistory," *Annual Review of Anthropology*, 29 (2000): 39–60, at 39.

[292] H. Demsetz, "Toward a Theory of Property Rights," *American Economic Review* 57, 2 (1967): 347–59, at 347. See also A. Alchian and H. Demsetz, "The Property Right Paradigm," *Journal of Economic History* 33 (1973): 16–27, at 17.

[293] See also R. C. Hunt, "Properties of Property: Conceptual Issues," in *Property in Economic Context*, ed. R C. Hunt and A. Gilman, Society for Economic Anthropology (Lanham: University Press of America, 1998), 7–28; Elinor Östrom, "An Agenda for the Study of Institu-

tions," *Public Choice* 48 (1986): 3–25; A. Stilz, "Nations, States, and Territory," *Ethics* 121, 3 (2011): 572–601.

[294] D. Blair Gibson, "Chiefdoms and the Emergence of Private Property in Land," *Journal of Anthropological Archaeology* 27 (2007): 46–62, at 46; Hunt, "Properties of Property," at 9; Bruce G. Carruthers and Laura Ariovich, "The Sociology of Property Rights," *Annual Review of Sociology* 30 (2004): 23–46.

[295] Östrom, *Governing the Commons*, 30; Hunt, "Properties of Property," at 11; S. Ciriacy-Wantrup and R. Bishop, "'Common Property' as a Concept in Natural Resources Policy," *Natural Resources Journal* 3 (1975): 713–27, at 714; Earle, "Archaeology, Property and Prehistory," at 51.

[296] Ciriacy-Wantrup and Bishop, "'Common Property' as a Concept," at 714.

[297] Neilson, *Terrier of Fleet*; "The Laws of Ine (688–694),"; Lambert, *Law and Order*, 71–72, 99, and chaps. 1 and 2. See Lisi Oliver, *Beginnings of English Law* (London: University of Toronto Press, 2002), for an alternative view arguing that Old English law was largely derived from Germanic antecedents.

[298] "From the Laws of Ethelbert, King of Kent (602–603?)," at 390–92.

[299] "The Laws of Ine (688–694)," at 403, paras. 40 and 42; see also Rosamond Faith, Andrew Fleming, and R. Kitchin, "Worthy Farms on the Edge of Dartmoor: A Preliminary Report," *Medieval Settlement Research* 22 (2007): 57. Lambert, *Law and Order*, 118–22.

[300] Andrew Fleming, *The Dartmoor Reaves: Investigating Prehistoric Land Divisions* (Oxford: Windgather, 2008), 84–90, 133, 156.

[301] See, for example, Barry Cunliffe, *Iron Age Communities in Britain* (London: Routledge, 2010), 251–57; Anthea Davies and Piers Dixon, "Reading the Pastoral Landscape: Palynological and Historical Evidence for the Impacts of Long-term Grazing on Wether Hill, Ingram, Northumberland," *Landscape History* 29 (2007): 35–47; Peter Herring, "Stepping onto the Commons: South-western Stone Rows," in *Monuments in the Landscape*, ed. Paul Rainbird (Stroud: Sutton, 2008), 79–88, at 86; Peter Herring and Peter Rose, *Bodmin Moor's Archaeological Heritage, Volume 1* (Swindon: English Heritage, 2001); Peter Herring, Nicholas Johnson, Andy Jones, et al. *Archaeology and Landscape at the Land's End, Cornwall: The West Penwith Surveys, 1982–2010* (Oxford: Oxbow, 2016); Cathy Stoertz, *Ancient Landscapes of the Yorkshire Wolds* (Swindon: English Heritage, 1997), 69–82; McOmish, Field, and Brown, *Field Archaeology of Salisbury Plain*, 102–3.

[302] D. A. Bullough, "Early Medieval Social Groupings: The Terminology of Kinship," *Past and Present* 45 (1969): 3–18; Charles-Edwards, "Kinship, Status"; Thomas Charles-Edwards, "Anglo-Saxon Kinship Revisited," in *The Anglo-Saxons from the Migration Period to the Eighth Century*, ed. John Hines (Woodbridge: Boydell and Brewer, 1997), 171–210; Faith, *English Peasantry*, 129–30; Chris Gosden, "Gifts and Kin in Early Iron Age Europe," *Man*, n.s. 20, 3 (1985): 475–93; Fergus Kelly, *Early Irish Farming* (Dublin: Dublin Institute for Advanced Studies, 1997), 412–14; Alice Rio, "Freedom and Unfreedom in Early Medieval *Francia*: The Evidence of the Legal Formulae," *Past and Present* 193 (2006): 7–40, at 37.

[303] For example, Millett, *Romanization*, 98.

[304] For example, Millett, *Romanization*, 98; Gerrard, *Ruin of Britain*, 144–45.

[305] See, for example, Martyn Allen, Tom Brindle, Tim Evans, et al., *The Rural Settlement of Roman Britain: An Online Resource* (2015), http://archaeologydataservice.ac.uk/archives/view/romangl/map.html.

[306] Jonathan Kissock and M. Anthony, "The Early Landscapes of Llandewi and Henllys, Gower," *Medieval Settlement Research Group Annual Report* 24 (2009): 70–77; Richard Hodges, *Roystone Grange: 6000 Years of a Peakland Landscape* (Stroud: History Press, 2006), 85–92.

[307] For example, H. P. R. Finberg, *Roman and Saxon Withington. A Study in Continuity* (Leicester: Leicester University Press, 1955); Glanville Jones, "Multiple Estates and Early Settlement," in *English Medieval Settlement*, ed. Peter Sawyer (London: Arnold, 1987): 9–34. For a more sceptical view see Chris Wickham, *Framing the Early Middle Ages* (Oxford: Oxford University Press, 2005), 347–48.

[308] "The Laws of Ine (688–694)," at 403–4.

[309] Neilson, *Terrier of Fleet*, xlix.

[310] Homans, "The Rural Sociology," at 39; Hoskins and Stamp, *The Common Lands*, 6; Edward Miller, *The Abbey and Bishopric of Ely* (Cambridge: Cambridge University Press, 1969), 13; Hamerow, *Early Medieval Settlements*, 129.

[311] Roberts, *Landscapes, Documents and Maps*, 166.

[312] For example, O. G. S. Crawford, *Wessex From the Air* (Oxford: Clarendon Press, 1928), 154; Andrew Fleming, "Territorial Patterns in Bronze Age Wessex," *Proceedings of the Prehistoric Society* 37, 1 (1971): 138–66, at 156–61; Fleming, *Dartmoor Reaves*, 91; Stoertz, *Ancient Landscapes of the Yorkshire Wolds*, 69–82; McOmish, Field, and Brown, *Field Archaeology of Salisbury Plain*, 64, 102–3;

Michael Parker Pearson, "Chieftains and Pastoralists in Neolithic and Bronze-Age Wessex," in *Monuments in the Landscape*, ed. P. Rainbird (Stroud: Sutton, 2008), 34–53; Michael Parker Pearson, "The Earlier Bronze Age," in *The Archaeology of Britain*, ed. J. Hunter and I. Ralston (London: Routledge, 2009), 103–25, at 120. For further instances see Oosthuizen, *Tradition and Transformation*, 20–34.

[313] Herring, "Stepping onto the Commons," at 86. See also Herring and Rose, *Bodmin Moor's Archaeological Heritage*; Herring, Johnson, Jones, et al., *Archaeology and Landscape*.

[314] For multiple further instances and bibliographic references, see Oosthuizen, *Tradition and Transformation*, 19–48.

[315] Millett, *Romanization*, 96–97, 197–99, 201.

[316] Gerrard, *Ruin of Roman Britain*, 143.

[317] See, for example, Wendy Davies, "Land and Power in Early Medieval Wales," *Past and Present* 81 (1978): 3–23, at 7–20; Reynolds, *Kingdoms and Communities*, 326.

[318] C. E. Stevens, "The Social and Economic Aspects of Rural Settlement," in *Rural Settlement in Roman Britain*, ed. C. Thomas (York: Council for British Archaeology, 1966), 108–28, at 108.

[319] J. F. Winkler, "Roman Law in Anglo-Saxon England," *Journal of Legal History* 13 (1992): 101–27, at 111n6, my addition; see also his 112n13.

[320] Rio, "Freedom and Unfreedom," at 37.

[321] McOmish, Field, and Brown, *Field Archaeology of Salisbury Plain*, 111.

[322] McOmish, Field, and Brown, *Field Archaeology of Salisbury Plain*, 111; Della Hooke, "Regional Variation in Southern and Central England in the Anglo-Saxon Period and its Relationship to Land Units and Settlement," in *Anglo-Saxon Settlements*, ed. Della Hooke (Oxford: Blackwell, 1988), 123–51, at 130; Barry Cunliffe, "Chalton, Hants.: The Evolution of a Landscape," *Antiquaries Journal* 53, 2 (1973): 173–90, at 183–88; David Hall, *Medieval Fields* (Princes Risborough: Shire, 1982), 54–55; G. Campbell, "The Preliminary Archaeobotanical Results from Anglo-Saxon West Cotton and Raunds," in *Environment and Economy in Anglo-Saxon England*, ed. J. Rackham (York: Council for British Archaeology, 1994), 65–82, at 65; Susan Oosthuizen, "New Light on the Origins of Open Field Farming?," *Medieval Archaeology* 49 (2005): 165–93; P. T. H. Unwin, "Townships and Early Fields in North Nottinghamshire," *Journal of Historical Geography* 9, 4 (1983): 341–46, at 344; A. E. Brown and Glenn Foard, "The Saxon Landscape: A Regional Perspective," in *The Archaeology of Landscape*, ed. Paul Everson and Tom Williamson

(Manchester: Manchester University Press, 1998), 67–94, at 74; Peter Addyman, "A Dark Age Settlement at Maxey, Northants.," *Medieval Archaeology* 8 (1964): 20–73, at 24; Catherine Hall and Jack Ravensdale, *The West Fields of Cambridge* (Cambridge: Cambridge Record Society, 1974).

[323] McOmish, Field, and Brown, *Field Archaeology of Salisbury Plain*, 111; Peter Fowler, *Farming in the First Millennium* (Cambridge: Cambridge University Press, 2002), 235–37.

[324] For detailed examples and bibliographic references see Susan Oosthuizen, "Medieval Field Systems and Settlement Nucleation: Common or Separate Origins?," in *The Landscapes of Anglo-Saxon England*, ed. Nicholas Higham (Woodbridge: Boydell and Brewer 2010), 108–31; Susan Oosthuizen, "Anglo-Saxon Fields," in *The Oxford Handbook of Anglo-Saxon Archaeology*, ed. David Hinton, Helena Hamerow, and Sally Crawford (Oxford: Oxford University Press, 2011), 377–401.

[325] Miles, *Barton Court Farm*, 14.

[326] S. Losco-Bradley and H. M. Wheeler, "Anglo-Saxon Settlement in the Trent Valley: Some Aspects," in *Studies in Late Anglo-Saxon Settlement*, ed. Margaret Faull (Oxford: Oxford Department for External Studies, 1984), 103–14, at 105.

[327] J. Bradley, M. Gaimster, and C. Haith, "Medieval Britain and Ireland, 1998," *Medieval Archaeology* 43 (1999): 226–302, at 251; Cunliffe, "Chalton, Hants.," at 183–88; M. Gaimster and J. Bradley, "Medieval Britain and Ireland, 2001," *Medieval Archaeology* 46 (2002): 125–264, at 242; Helena Hamerow, *Excavations at Mucking, Volume 2: The Anglo-Saxon Settlement* (London: English Heritage and British Museum Press, 1993), 94; Carenza Lewis, Patrick Mitchell-Fox, and Christopher Dyer, *Village, Hamlet and Field* (Manchester: Manchester University Press, 1997), 92; Hey, *Yarnton*, 37–39; Yorke, *Wessex in the Early Middle Ages*, 264–65; Helena Hamerow, Chris Hayden, G. Hey, et al., "Anglo-Saxon and Earlier Settlement near Drayton Road, Sutton Courtenay, Berkshire," *Archaeological Journal* 164, 1 (2007): 109–86, at 115.

[328] Some of many examples include: Royal Commission on Historic Monuments (England), *West Cambridgeshire* (London: HMSO, 1968), xxx; Christopher Taylor and Peter Fowler, "Roman Fields into Medieval Furlongs?," in *Early Land Allotment in the British Isles*, ed. H. C. Bowen and Peter Fowler, BAR British Series, 48 (Oxford: British Archaeological Reports, 1978), 159–62, at 159; Maurice Beresford and John Hurst, "Wharram Percy: A Case Study in Microtopography," in *English Medieval Settlement*, ed. Peter Sawyer (London:

Arnold, 1979), 52–85, at 82; June Sheppard, *The Origins and Evolution of Field and Settlement Patterns in the Herefordshire Manor of Marden*, Department of Geography Occasional Paper, 15 (London: Queen Mary College, 1979) 33; RCHM(E), *Central Northamptonshire*, lxii; Steven Bassett, "Medieval Lichfield: A Topographical Review," *Transactions of the Staffordshire Archaeological and Historical Society*, 22 (1980–81): 93–121; A. Nash, "The Medieval Fields of Strettington, West Sussex, and the Evolution of Land Division," *Geografiska Annaler* 1982B, 1 (1982): 41–49, at 42; Steven Bassett, "Beyond the Edge of Excavation: The Topographical Context of Goltho," in *Studies in Medieval History Presented to R. H. C. Davis*, ed. H. Mayr-Harting and R. I. Moore (London: Hambledon, 1985), 21–40, at 32–34; Della Hooke, "Early Forms of Open Field Agriculture in England," *Geografiska Annaler*, 70B (1988): 121–31, at 123–25; Hooke, "Regional Variation," at 131; *Rackham, History of the Countryside*, 158; E. J. Bull, "The Bi-axial Landscape of Prehistoric Buckinghamshire," *Records of Buckinghamshire* 35 (1993): 11–27, at 16; A. E. Brown, "Burton Lazars, Leicestershire: A Planned Medieval Landscape?," *Landscape History*, 18 (1996): 31–45, at 43; Oosthuizen, "Prehistoric Fields into Medieval Furlongs?"; M. Gaimster and J. Bradley, "Medieval Britain and Ireland, 2000," *Medieval Archaeology* 45 (2001): 233–379, at 294–95; Upex, "Landscape Continuity," at 87–94; Fowler, *Farming in the First Millennium*, 235–37; Oosthuizen, *Landscapes Decoded*, 68–90.

[329] Jonathan Kissock, "'God Made Nature and Men made Towns': Post-conquest and Pre-conquest Villages in Pembrokeshire," in *Landscape and Settlement in Medieval Wales*, ed. Nancy Edwards (Oxford: Oxbow, 1997), 123–38.

[330] A. S. Kubat, "The Morphological History of Istanbul," *Urban Morphology* 31 (1999): 28–41, at 38–39.

[331] G. F. Cruchley, *New Plan of London Improved to 1827 Including the East and West India Docks* (London: Cruchley, 1827), http://mapco.net/cruchley/cruchley.htm; George Arkell, "Map of the Jewish Settlement in London," in *The Jew in London*, ed. C. Russell and H. S. Lewis (London: Fisher Unwin, 1900), via London Jewish Cultural Centre, https://www.jewsfww.london/map.php.

[332] A. P. M. Wright and C. P. Lewis, "Childerley: Parish Essay," in *A History of the County of Cambridge and the Isle of Ely: Volume 9, Chesterton, Northstowe, and Papworth Hundreds*, ed. A. P. M. Wright and C. P. Lewis (London: Institute of Historical Research, 1989), 39–48; Royal Commission on Historic Monuments (England), *An Inventory of the Historical Monuments in the County of Cam-*

bridgeshire, Volume 1, West Cambridgeshire (London: HMSO, 1968), 210–29. For modern examples in parts of eastern Prussia, Silesia, and Pomerania after the second world war, see Keith Lowe, *Savage Continent. Europe in the Aftermath of World War II* (London: Viking, 2012), 221–24, 230–34.

[333] Benjamin Gearey, D. Charman, and M. Kent, "Palaeoecological Evidence for the Prehistoric Settlement of Bodmin Moor, Cornwall, Southwest England. Part II: Land Use Changes from the Neolithic to the Present," *Journal of Archaeological Science* 27 (2000): 493–508, at 506.

[334] Davies and Dixon, "Reading the Pastoral Landscape."

[335] Alison Deegan and Glenn Foard, *Mapping Ancient Landscapes in Northamptonshire* (Swindon: English Heritage 2007), 133; Oliver Rackham, *Trees and Woodland in the British Landscape* (London: Phoenix, 1994), 145; Cunliffe, "Chalton, Hants.," at 183; McOmish, Field, and Brown, *Field Archaeology of Salisbury Plain*, 64, 102–3, 107; Cunliffe, *Iron Age Communities*, 51; Royal Commission on Historic Monuments (England), *Iron Age and Roman Monuments in the Gloucestershire Cotswolds* (London: HMSO, 1976), 83b; Fleming, "Territorial Patterns," at 156–61; Fleming, *Dartmoor Reaves*, 91, 133; Parker Pearson, "The Earlier Bronze Age," at 120; Crawford, *Wessex From the Air*, 154; Stoertz, *Ancient Landscapes of the Yorkshire Wolds*, 69–82; Herring, "Stepping onto the Commons," at 86; Oosthuizen, *Landscapes Decoded*; Davison, *Evolution of Settlement*; Oosthuizen, *Anglo-Saxon Fenland*, 10–11, 90–93.

[336] Susan Oosthuizen, "Beyond Hierarchy: The Archaeology of Collective Governance," *World Archaeology* 45 (2013): 714–29. For further detailed instances and bibliographic references, see Oosthuizen, *Tradition and Transformation*, 24–39. Hefting—the exploitation of cattle and sheep's natural territorial instincts to confine them to one or another section of open pasture—is nonetheless a form of grazing exploited under rights of common.

[337] For example, Timothy Darvill, *Prehistoric Britain from the Air: A Study of Time, Space and Society* (Cambridge: Cambridge University Press, 1996), 30–31; Martin Jones, "A Feast of Beltane? Reflections on the Rich Danebury Harvests," in *Communities and Connections: Essays in Honour of Barry Cunliffe*, ed. Chris Gosden, Helena Hamerow, P. de Jersey, and Gary Lock (Oxford: Oxford University Press, 2007): 142–53; Gary Lock, "Wessex Hillforts after Danebury: Exploring Boundaries," in *Communities and Connections*, 341–56; Cunliffe, *Iron Age Communities*, 382, 379–82; Francis Pryor, "The Welland Valley as a Cultural Boundary Zone: An Example of Long-

term History," in *Through Wet and Dry*, ed. Tom Lane and John Coles, Lincolnshire Archaeology and Heritage Reports Series, 5 (Sleaford: Heritage Trust of Lincolnshire, 2002), 18–32, at 20; Roger Mercer, "Hambledon Hill," *British Archaeology* 107 (2009): 38–43; Andrew Payne, Mark Corney, and Barry Cunliffe, *The Wessex Hillforts Project* (Swindon: English Heritage, 2006), 156; McOmish, Field, and Brown, *Field Archaeology of Salisbury Plain*, 73, 60; Neil Sharples, *Social Relations in Later Prehistory* (Oxford: Oxford University Press, 2010), 52, 308; Hamerow, *Early Medieval Settlements*, 124; Susan Oosthuizen, "Archaeology, Common Rights, and the Origins of Anglo-Saxon Identity," *Early Medieval Europe* 19 (2011): 153–81.

[338] Alan Everitt, "Common Land," in *Rural England: An Illustrated History of the Landscape*, ed. Joan Thirsk (Oxford: Oxford University Press, 2002), 210–35, at 216; Finberg, *Withington*, 37; Margaret Gelling, *The West Midlands in the Early Middle Ages* (Leicester: Leicester University Press, 1992), 64; Michael Costen, "The Late Saxon Landscape," in *Aspects of the Medieval Landscape of Somerset*, ed. Michael Aston (Taunton: Somerset County Council, 1988), 33–48, at 41; Nicholas Higham, *A Frontier Landscape* (Macclesfield: Windgather, 2004), 30; W. Ford, "Some Settlement Patterns in the Central Region of the Warwickshire Avon," in *English Medieval Settlement*, ed. Peter Sawyer (London: Arnold, 1987), 143–63, at 148; Oliver Rackham, "Woods, Hedges and Ditches," in *Aspects of the Medieval Landscape of Somerset*, ed. Michael Aston (Taunton: Somerset County Council, 1988) 13–32, at 25.

[339] Hoskins and Stamp, *The Common Lands*, 7, 24; Andrew Fleming, "The Quest for Territorial Pattern," in *The Archaeology of Landscape*, ed. Paul Everson and Tom Williamson (Manchester: Manchester University Press, 1998), 42–66, at 56; Neilson, *Priory of Bilsington Kent*, 3–7, 34.

[340] Jones, "Multiple Estates," 29–30. Recent archaeological investigation at the site of Aldborough appears to confirm Jones' interpretation: Martin Wainwright, "Archaeologist Digs into Grandad's Tale to Uncover Lost Yorkshire Amphitheatre," *The Guardian*, August 17, 2011. http://www.guardian.co.uk/culture/2011/aug/17/lost-yorkshire-amphitheatre-aldborough.

[341] Rackham, *History of the Countryside*, 67.

[342] Kelly, *Early Irish Farming*, 407. See also Gosden, "Gifts and Kin"; Oosthuizen, "Archaeology, Common Rights, and the Origins of Anglo-Saxon Identity"; Oosthuizen, *Tradition and Transformation*, 160–62.

[343] Wendy Davies, *Wales in the Early Middle Ages* (Leicester:

Leicester University Press, 1982), 63; Glanville Jones "Early Customary Tenures in Wales and Open-field Agriculture," in *The Origins of Open-Field Agriculture*, ed. Trevor Rowley (London: Croom Helm, 1981), 202–55, at 202, 207; Kelly, *Early Irish Farming*, 406–7, 447, 656; C. Trench, " Peasant Agriculture in Medieval Gwynedd," *Folk Life* 13 (1975): 24–37, at 26.

[344] Faith, *English Peasantry*, 48, 89–90.

[345] Faith, *English Peasantry*, chaps. 4 and 5; Neilson, *Terrier of Fleet*.

[346] Rackham, *History of the Countryside*, 73–77.

[347] John Coles and Bryony Coles, *Sweet Track to Glastonbury* (London: Thames and Hudson, 1986), 55–56, 77, 85, 105; T. C. Lethbridge, "Investigations of the Ancient Causeway in the Fen between Fordy and Little Thetford," *Proceedings of the Cambridge Antiquarian Society* 35 (1934), 86–89; Francis Pryor, *The Flag Fen Basin. Archaeology and Environment of a Fenland Landscape* (Swindon: English Heritage, 2001), 152, 171.

[348] Sharples, *Social Relations*, 204–5.

[349] Oliver Rackham, *Woodlands* (London: Collins, 2010), 41, 68; Rackham, "Woods, Hedges and Ditches," at 18, 75; McOmish, Field, and Brown, *Field Archaeology of Salisbury Plain*, 97.

[350] Richard Hodges, *The Anglo-Saxon Achievement* (London: Duckworth, 1989), 36. See also Philip Dixon, "How Saxon is the Saxon House?," in *Structural Reconstruction*, ed. P. J. Drury (Oxford, Oxford University Press, 1982), 275–78; S. James, A. Marshall and Martin Millett, "An Early Medieval Building Tradition," *Archaeological Journal* 141 (1984): 182–215; Martin Welch, "Rural Settlement Patterns in the Early and Middle Anglo-Saxon Period," *Landscape History* 7 (1985): 13–25, at 15–16.

[351] B. Hayden and A. Cannon, "The Corporate Group as an Archaeological Unit," *Journal of Anthropological Archaeology* 1 (1982): 132–58, at 134.

[352] R. M. Netting, "What Alpine Peasants Have in Common: Observations on Communal Tenure in a Swiss Village," *Human Ecology* 4 (1976): 135–46; Östrom, "An Agenda," at 6; Östrom, *Governing the Commons*, 38, 90; F. Lu, "The Common Property Regime of the Huaorani Indians of Ecuador: Implications and Challenges to Conservation," *Human Ecology* 29 (2001): 425–47, at 428; L. M. Ruttan, "Closing the Commons: Cooperation for Gain or Restraint?," *Human Ecology* 26 (1998): 43–66, at 59, 62, 77; P. Trawick, "Successfully Governing the Commons: Principles of Social Organization in an Andean Irrigation System," *Human Ecology* 29 (2001): 1–25,

at 13; E. P. Thompson, "The Moral Economy of the English Crowd in the Eighteenth Century," *Past and Present* 50 (1971): 76–136; Reynolds, *Kingdoms and Communities*.

[353] Faith, *English Peasantry*, 117.

[354] Reynolds, "Medieval *Origines Gentium*," at 381.

[355] Neilson, *Terrier of Fleet*, li; Oosthuizen, *Tradition and Transformation*, 1–14; Oosthuizen, *Anglo-Saxon Fenland*, xiv–xix and chap. 4.

[356] Della Hooke, "Early Cotswold Woodland," *Journal of Historical Geography* 4 (1978): 333–41, at 335.

[357] 958AD S679, King Efgar to Oscytel, grant of ten hides at Sutton, Nottinghamshire, http://www.esawyer.org.uk/about/index.html.

[358] Hoskins and Stamp, *The Common Lands*, 7–8.

[359] Neilson, *Terrier of Fleet*; Oosthuizen, *Anglo-Saxon Fenland*, chaps. 4 and 5; Susan Oosthuizen, "Beyond Hierarchy: Archaeology, Common Rights and Social Identity", *World Archaeology* 48, 3 (2016): 383–91.

[360] Wendy Davies and Hayo Vierck, "The Contexts of the Tribal Hidage: Social Aggregates and Settlement Patterns," *Frühmittelalterliche Studien* 8 (1974): 223–93, at 224; see also for example, Davies, "Land and Power," 14; Faith, *English Peasantry*, 147, 2; Lewis, et al., *Village, Hamlet and Field*, 184.

[361] Fowler, *Farming in the First Millennium*, 224, my addition.

[362] Roberts, *Landscapes, Documents and Maps*, 166, my addition.

[363] Examples of such landscapes researched in depth include in particular Everitt, *Continuity and Colonization*, and Oosthuizen, *Anglo-Saxon Fenland*. See also Neilson, *Terrier of Fleet*; Neilson, *Priory of Bilsington*, 3–7, 34; Reynolds, *Kingdoms and Communities*, 111, 138–39; Davies and Vierck, "Contexts of the Tribal Hidage"; Ford, "Some Settlement Patterns"; Roffe, "The Historical Context"; Finberg, "Anglo-Saxon England to 1042," 404–10, 497; Faith, *English Peasantry*, 30; Everitt, "Common Land," 215; Pauline Stafford, *The East Midlands in the Early Middle Ages* (Leicester: Leicester University Press, 1985), 8.

[364] Everitt, *Continuity and Colonization*; Oosthuizen, *Anglo-Saxon Fenland*; Stoertz, *Ancient Landscapes of the Yorkshire Wolds.*

[365] Davies and Dixon, "Reading the Pastoral Landscape"; McOmish, Field, and Brown, *Field Archaeology of Salisbury Plain*; Fleming, *Dartmoor Reaves*; H. S. A. Fox, *Dartmoor's Alluring Uplands* (Exeter: University of Exeter Press, 2012); Herring, "Stepping onto the Commons"; Herring and Rose, *Bodmin Moor's Archaeological Heritage, Volume 1*; Herring, Johnson, Jones, et al., *Archaeology and Landscape*.

[366] Oosthuizen, *Anglo-Saxon Fenland*, chap. 4.

[367] Oosthuizen, "Beyond Hierarchy: Archaeology, Common Rights and Social Identity."

[368] Newman, "Sutton Hoo before Rædwald," at 505, my addition.

[369] Braudel, "*La Longue Durée*"; Holling, "Understanding the Complexity," at 397; Östrom, "An Agenda," at 5. See also Hayden and Cannon, "The Corporate Group," at 134.

[370] See, for example, Östrom, "An Agenda"; Östrom, *Governing the Commons*, 88–102.

[371] Cunliffe, *Iron Age Communities,* 681. For similar formulations see Braudel, *The Mediterranean* and *The Identity of France*; Bourdieu, *Theory of Practice*; Holling, "Understanding the Complexity"; Gunderson and Holling, *Panarchy*; Folke, "Resilience"; Plielinger and Bieling, *Resilience and the Cultural Landscape*. Readers may have come across Garrett Hardin, "The Tragedy of the Commons" (*Science*, n.s. 162, 3859 (1968): 1243–48) which argued that areas under common rights would inevitably fail since exploitation for short-term individual self-interest would always outweigh collective ideals of long-term sustainability. That paper was based on a fallacy: the resources it defined were those held under public rights of property not common rights, and the paper was convincingly debunked by Ciriacy-Wantrup and Bishop, "'Common Property' as a Concept."

[372] Martin, *Cruciform Brooch,* 78. See also Hodges, *Anglo-Saxon Achievement*; Williamson, "East Anglia's Character."

[373] Martin, *Cruciform Brooch*, 88–89, 110, 126, 143, 232.

[374] Martin, *Cruciform Brooch*, 223–32.

[375] Martin, *Cruciform Brooch*, 168–71, 187.

[376] For example, Martin, *Cruciform Brooch*, 163.

Index

Printed and bound by CPI Group (UK) Ltd, Croydon, CR0 4YY

25/03/2025

14647339-0005